1994

Happy Birthday, La
from Grandma Bremer

low fat cooking

can simmer them in a little stock and then, instead of thickening the sauce with a blend of flour and fat, purée some of the ingredients, the stock, and the vegetables, to act as an integral and tasty thickening agent.

You can make cream soups by using skimmed milk and low-fat yogurt, which let all the flavors of the vegetables come through. Compensate for any loss of dairy flavor by a little sleight of hand, increasing the proportion of fresh and dried herbs and spices. A few gratings of nutmeg in a cauliflower or Jerusalem artichoke soup, a hint of ground coriander or chopped coriander leaves in a butter bean soup, a generous hand with the chopped mint in a corn soup – the flavor permutations are endless.

meat and fish

A well-planned low-fat and low-cholesterol program calls for a careful balancing act in the choice, and frequency of serving, of meat and fish.

The equation is simple. Meat, even lean meat, contains a significant amount of saturated fat, while poultry and game – take your choice from chicken, turkey, rabbit, pheasant – have markedly lower levels. The predominant oils in fish are polyunsaturates, which are present in small amounts in white fish of all kinds – cod, haddock, and sole, for example – and higher proportions in oily fish such as mackerel, her-

ring, salmon, and trout.

When you do choose meat, buy lean cuts, and even then cut off all visible and excess fat. Place meat for roasting on a rack in the roasting pan, so that the fat drops below it and the meat is not left swimming in it. If necessary, brush meat for broiling with a polyunsaturated oil or margarine, and dry-fry ground meat or cubes of meat in a non-stick pan, then pour off the fat and wipe away the greasiness with paper towels.

If you cook or serve the meat with a full complement of vegetables, pulses, and grains, you will find that you can imperceptibly but significantly reduce the portion sizes – thus balancing both the health factors and your budget. Our suggestions for marinated strips of lean beef stir-fried with nuts and vegetables, or wafer-thin slices of veal or chicken breast enclosing a blend of carrot and brown rice are just two examples of healthful meat dishes.

When it comes to choosing poultry, it is best to select from the perhaps less attractive and less fatty birds available. Discard any loose fat inside the bird, and, since much of the remaining fat will be in and close to the skin, either discard the skin or prick it all over to release the fat through drainage channels. If you are served a portion of roast chicken with crisp, golden skin, so much higher in fat than the lean meat, take a deep breath and leave it – for the birds.
crispy, golden skin, so much higher in fat than the lean meat, take a deep breath and leave it – for the birds.

ABOVE **Pulses is the collective name given to beans, lentils and peas. A wealth of minerals,** vitamins and unrefined carbohydrates are found in pulses.

ABOVE **The benefits of fruit as a substitute for refined fatty desserts are numerous. Not only do they have no fat, but** they supply essential vitamins, minerals and fibre.

pulses and grains

A gradual change to a low-fat and low-cholesterol program almost inevitably leads to a closer look at all the exciting possibilities offered by the whole range of pulses, grains, and vegetables. This results in the added health benefit of increasing your consumption of dietary fiber.

Take the spotlight away from meat and it falls on whole-grain fillings, accompaniments and toppings with a delicious range of textures and flavors all their own. And with so much variety that one scarcely knows where to begin.

desserts and baking

The use, in moderation, of polyunsaturated cooking fats and oils puts the irresistible aroma of baking and the treasured variety of our regional dishes – no matter where we might live – right on target for a healthy regime.

Where dietary cholesterol is concerned, eggs are sharply divided between whites, which have none, and yolks, which have a very high amount – almost the highest concentration

in fact, of any foodstuff. So it makes sense to save up the yolks for a friend who is not cholesterol-counting, or make mayonnaise to sell at a bazaar, and whip up the whites into delectable meringues filled with fruit purée and served with low-fat yogurt or low-fat cheese.

White sugar and some types of soft brown sugar are re-fined sugars which provide no vitamins and few minerals, only calories. If a recipe calls for sweeteners, it is preferable to use natural sweeteners where possible, the less refined sugars such as light and dark muscovado, honey or con-centrated apple juice.

Whether you are just considering changing the eating pattern of a lifetime, or have been advised by a doctor to do so, or are seeking inspiration for an ever-increasing number of suitable dishes, we hope the following recipes will help you. We hope that they will encourage you to think positively, and consider all the exciting flavor and texture combinations at your fingertips. We promise that you will never look back.

breakfast

. . . .

Bowls of steaming hot cereal, made all the more delicious and nourishing by the addition of fresh and dried fruits, oat pancakes filled with a tasty blend of cottage cheese and raisins, ramekin dishes of baked haddock and cottage cheese (an update of a traditional fish dish), a fruit, nut, and yogurt meal-in-a-glass for those in a hurry — in these and other breakfast dishes we show you the healthy way to get the day off to an energy-packed start.

Many of the recipes in this section can be prepared in moments; others can be prepared in the evening, ready to pop in the oven or a non-stick frying pan the following morning. They all set out to prove that when time is of the essence, as it is in so many households first thing in the morning, the family's health can still be paramount.

apricot granola

You can vary the granola mixture in many ways, substituting different nuts and seeds and using other dried fruits in place of the apricots. Do not store the granola until it has completely cooled, or it will sweat and the ingredients will soften.

Preparation time: 10 minutes
Cooking time: 25 minutes, plus cooling
SERVES 8–10

3 tbsp sunflower oil • 6 tbsp clear honey
1 cup rolled oats • ⅔ cup rolled jumbo oats
⅓ cup hazelnuts, chopped • ⅛ cup sunflower seeds
⅙ cup sesame seeds • 1 cup dried apricots, chopped

Set the oven to 325°F. Melt the oil and the honey in a saucepan over a low heat. Stir in the oats, chopped nuts, and seeds, mix well, and immediately remove from the heat.

Spread the mixture on a cookie sheet and bake in the oven for 25 minutes, stirring from time to time with a wooden spoon. Remove the cookie tray from the oven, stir in the chopped apricots, and set aside to cool. When the mixture has thoroughly cooled, store it in an airtight jar in the refrigerator.

You can serve the granola with a tempting variety of dairy products and fruit juices. Try it with buttermilk, or plain low-fat yogurt mixed half-and-half with orange, apple, or pineapple juice, or with fruit juice alone.*

FOOD VALUES	TOTAL FAT	SATURATED FAT	CHOLESTEROL	ENERGY
TOTAL	104 g	11.5 g	0 mg	2095 kcals/ 8791 kj
PER PORTION (8)	13 g	1.5 g	0 mg	262 kcals/ 1099 kj
(10)	10 g	1 g	0 mg	210 kcals/ 879 kj

*NOT INCLUDED IN NUTRITIONAL ANALYSIS

honey-poached figs

This recipe comes from Greece, where round whole semi-dried figs are readily available. You can buy them in some healthfood shops.

Preparation time: 5 minutes
Cooking time: 20 minutes, plus cooling
SERVES 4

1 cinnamon stick • 3 tbsp clear honey
1 cup water or orange juice • 2½ cups semi-dried figs
1 cup plain low-fat yogurt • 4 tbsp chopped walnuts

Put the cinnamon stick, honey, and water or orange juice into a shallow pan and bring to the boil. Add the figs and simmer for 20 minutes, turning them occasionally with a wooden spoon. Remove from the heat and set aside to cool.

Lift out the figs with a slotted spoon. Stir the yogurt into the poaching liquid, blending it thoroughly. Pour into a serving bowl and stir in the figs. Sprinkle on the chopped walnuts just before serving.

FOOD VALUES	TOTAL FAT	SATURATED FAT	CHOLESTEROL	ENERGY
TOTAL	57 g	6 g	10 mg	1098 kcals/ 4592 kj
PER PORTION	14 g	1.5 g	2.5 mg	275 kcals/ 1148 kj

potato cakes

If you prepare the spicy potato cake mixture in advance, it can be cooked quickly the next morning in a non-stick pan. The pancakes are especially good served with grilled tomatoes.

Preparation time: 15 minutes, plus soaking
Cooking time: 10 minutes
SERVES 4

1½ lb potatoes, peeled or scraped
2 tbsp wholewheat flour, plus extra for dusting
2 tbsp 100% bran cereal, crushed • 1 small onion, grated
2 tbsp chopped parsley • 1–2 tsp curry powder • salt
3 tbsp low-fat milk • oil, for brushing
GARNISH
parsley sprigs

Soak the potatoes in cold water for about 30 minutes to remove some of the starch. Drain, rinse, and dry them, and then grate coarsely into a bowl.

Stir in the flour, bran flakes, onion, parsley, and curry powder to taste, and season with salt. Lastly, stir in the milk and shape the mixture into a round. Divide it into 8 equal-sized pieces. Brush your hands with flour, and shape the pieces into flat rounds. Sprinkle the potato cakes with wholewheat flour to cover them on all sides.

Lightly brush a non-stick frying pan with oil, and heat it over a medium heat. Fry the potato cakes for 4–5 minutes on each side, until they are evenly brown. Serve them hot, garnished with parsley.

FOOD VALUES	TOTAL FAT	SATURATED FAT	CHOLESTEROL	ENERGY
TOTAL	10 g	1.5 g	4 mg	880 kcals/ 3720 kj
PER PORTION	2.5 g	0.5 g	1 mg	220 kcals/ 930 kj

hungarian oat pancakes

Oat pancakes, like any others, freeze well, so it is a good idea to make a double batch and store some of them.

Preparation time: 10 minutes
Cooking time: 30 minutes
SERVES 4

⅔ cup rolled oats • ⅓ cup (generous) wholewheat flour
pinch salt • 1 tsp grated orange rind • ⅝ cup orange juice
⅝ cup skimmed milk • 2 egg whites, lightly beaten
oil, for brushing • 2 tbsp light unrefined brown sugar
FILLING
1 cup low-fat cottage cheese • 1¼ cup seedless raisins
1 tsp grated orange rind
GARNISH
orange sections

In a bowl, mix together the oats, flour, salt, and orange rind. Gradually pour on the orange juice and milk, beating constantly. Fold in the egg whites. Lightly brush a non-stick omelet pan with oil, and heat it over medium heat. Pour in just enough of the batter to cover the base, and tip the pan to spread it evenly. Cook the pancake until it bubbles and is browned on the under side. Flip or toss it and cook on the other side.

Cook the remainder of the batter in the same way. Depending on the size of the pan, the mixture should make 8–10 pancakes.

Mix together the cheese, raisins, and orange rind for the filling. Spread about 2 tbsp of the mixture in the center of each pancake and roll them up. You can prepare the pancakes to this stage, cover, and store in the refrigerator overnight.

Set the broiler to medium. Arrange the pancakes in a flame-proof dish, and sprinkle them with the sugar. Grill until the sugar caramelizes, then serve hot, decorated with the orange sections.

FOOD VALUES	TOTAL FAT	SATURATED FAT	CHOLESTEROL	ENERGY
TOTAL	15 g	4 g	14 mg	1400 kcals/ 5947 kj
PER PORTION	4 g	1 g	4 mg	350 kcals/ 1487 kj

baked haddock ramekins

A tasty and filling hot dish which you can prepare the night before, all ready to be baked in the morning.

Preparation time: 10 minutes
Cooking time: 20 minutes, plus pre-cooking fish
SERVES 4

1 cup cooked smoked haddock, skinned, boned, and flaked
1 cup low-fat cottage cheese with chives
¼ lb button mushrooms, trimmed and chopped
1 tsp grated lemon rind • 2 tsp lemon juice
1 tbsp chopped parsley • 1 small egg, beaten
grated nutmeg • pepper • oil, for brushing
GARNISH
watercress sprigs

Mix together the flaked haddock, cottage cheese, and mushrooms. Stir in the lemon rind, lemon juice, and parsley, and then the beaten egg. Season the mixture with nutmeg and pepper.

Divide the mixture between 4 small ramekin dishes, lightly brushed with oil. Level the tops and cover the dishes with foil. If they are not to be cooked right away, store them in the refrigerator.

Set the oven to 350°F. Stand the dishes in a roasting pan with enough warm water to come half way up the sides. Cook in the oven for 20 minutes, until the mixture is set.

Garnish each dish with a sprig of watercress, and serve hot with wholewheat toast.*

FOOD VALUES	TOTAL FAT	SATURATED FAT	CHOLESTEROL	ENERGY
TOTAL	22 g	8 g	370 mg	583 kcals/ 2460 kj
PER PORTION	6 g	2 g	93 mg	146 kcals/ 615 kj

*NOT INCLUDED IN NUTRITIONAL ANALYSIS

Baked Haddock Ramekins

banana cocktail

This is a nourishing "spoon drink" to serve to people caught up in the morning rush. The honey and citrus fruits compensate for any loss of dairy flavor that comes from using skimmed milk.

Preparation time: 10 minutes, plus overnight soaking
SERVES 4

1⅓ cup rolled oats • ¾ cup skimmed milk
4 tbsp clear honey
2 large eating apples, peeled, cored, and grated
2 medium bananas, thinly sliced • juice of 1 lemon
juice of 1 orange • 2 tsp grated orange rind
1¼ cup plain low-fat yogurt
GARNISH
4 tsp dark muscovado or brown sugar
2 tbsp fresh or frozen berries, or orange sections

Soak the oats in skimmed milk overnight. In the morning stir in all the remaining ingredients, and divide the mixture between 4 individual serving glasses, such as sundae glasses.

Sprinkle 1 tsp of sugar over each glass, and decorate it with whatever fruit is available. Scottish oatcakes, available from some delicatessens, make a very good accompaniment.*

FOOD VALUES	TOTAL FAT	SATURATED FAT	CHOLESTEROL	ENERGY
TOTAL	13 g	3.5 g	15.5 mg	1399 kcals/ 5943 kj
PER PORTION	3 g	1 g	4 mg	350 kcals/ 1486 kj

*NOT INCLUDED IN NUTRITIONAL ANALYSIS

fruit compote with yogurt

A refreshing blend of flavors to start the day. The fruit can also be served with *fromage frais* or with smetana, a yogurt-like product very low in fat.

Preparation time: 15 minutes, plus cooling
Cooking time: 20 minutes
SERVES 4

⅝ cup dried prunes • ¾ cup dried apricots
⅝ cup dried pears • 1¼ cup orange juice
⅝ cup water • strip lemon rind
4 tbsp yogurt or *fromage frais* • 2 tbsp chopped walnuts

Place the prunes, apricots, pears, orange juice, water, and lemon rind in a saucepan, and bring to the boil. Cover and simmer for 15 minutes. Set aside to cool.

Serve the fruit warm or chilled, with a spoonful of yogurt or *fromage frais*, and sprinkle with walnuts.

FOOD VALUES	TOTAL FAT	SATURATED FAT	CHOLESTEROL	ENERGY
TOTAL	29 g	2 g	2 mg	904 kcals/ 3815 kj
PER PORTION	7 g	0.5 g	0.5 mg	226 kcals/ 954 kj

starters

An appetizer or soup plays a very important part in a two- or three-course meal. It serves as the overture to everything that is to follow: delighting the eye, exciting the palate, whetting yet never dulling the appetite, and both contrasting with and complementing the main dish. It's quite a challenge!

The recipes in this section meet that challenge with gusto. They include taste-bud-tingling soups and chowders that owe nothing to fat-laden dairy flavors and everything to the stimulating blends of fresh and dried vegetables, herbs, and spices. By way of contrast there are also crisp fruit and vegetable salads presented with style. Make your opening selection from partnerships as varied as curly endive and — possibly home-grown — alfalfa shoots, high-fiber corn kernels criss crossed with tender green beans, and a soft spreadable pâté of eggplants and mushrooms. They all bring health-consciousness right to the front of the agenda.

Broiled Fruits with Honey

broiled fruits with honey

Present citrus fruits in a different way – broiled and served piping hot in a golden honey sauce.

Preparation time: 15 minutes
Cooking time: 5 minutes
SERVES 4

2 grapefruit, peeled and sectioned
3 oranges, peeled and sectioned • 6 tbsp clear honey
2 tbsp brown unrefined sugar
1 tbsp polyunsaturated margarine
GARNISH
2 tbsp chopped mint

Set the broiler to high. Place the grapefruit and orange segments in a single layer in a flameproof dish.

In a small pan, heat the honey, sugar, and margarine until it has melted. Stir to blend it well, and pour it over the fruit.

Broil the fruit for about 4 minutes, until the sections are just beginning to brown and the sauce is bubbling. Sprinkle with the mint and serve at once. Chilled plain low-fat yogurt makes a good accompaniment.*

FOOD VALUES	TOTAL FAT	SATURATED FAT	CHOLESTEROL	ENERGY
TOTAL	13 g	2 g	1 mg	1015 kcals/ 4315 kj
PER PORTION	3 g	0.5 g	0.25 mg	254 kcals/ 1079 kj

*NOT INCLUDED IN NUTRITIONAL ANALYSIS

nutty cucumber boats

A perfect first course for a hot summer day, or for an *alfresco* meal. You could add texture and flavor – fiber too – by mixing 2 tablespoons of seedless raisins into the filling.

Preparation time: 10 minutes
SERVES 4

8″ piece cucumber, cut in half lengthwise
⅓ cup pine nuts toasted • ¼ cup cashew nuts, toasted
½ cup cottage cheese
4 medium tomatoes, skinned, seeded, and chopped
2 tsp chopped dill • 1 tsp chopped mint
GARNISH
lettuce leaves • dill sprigs

Scoop out the centers of the cucumber pieces and cut into 2″ pieces.

Mix together the nuts, cheese, tomatoes, dill, and mint. Spoon into each cucumber wedge.

Arrange the cucumber "boats" on a bed of lettuce leaves, garnish with dill sprigs, and serve at once.

> Do not mix the filling more than a few minutes before serving, or the nuts will become soggy and lose their crispness.

FOOD VALUES	TOTAL FAT	SATURATED FAT	CHOLESTEROL	ENERGY
TOTAL	49 g	6 g	5 mg	681 kcals/ 2824 kj
PER PORTION	12 g	1.5 g	1.25 mg	170 kcals/ 706 kj

watercress soup

Watercress is not only a versatile and slightly acidic green vegetable, it is also rich in Vitamin A, iodine, iron, and calcium.

Preparation time: 10 minutes
Cooking time: 25 minutes
SERVES 4

1 tbsp polyunsaturated margarine • 1 medium onion, chopped
2 bunches watercress, trimmed
½ lb potatoes, peeled or scraped and diced
1½ cups vegetable stock • 1¼ cups low-fat milk
pinch cayenne pepper • salt
GARNISH
wholewheat croutons, toasted (optional)

Melt the margarine in a large saucepan, add the onion, and cook over medium heat for 2–3 minutes to soften.

Reserve 4 sprigs of watercress for garnish, and chop the remainder. Add the watercress to the onion along with the potato. Cook gently for 3–4 minutes, stirring occasionally. Add the stock, bring to the boil, cover, and simmer for 15–20 minutes, or until potatoes are tender.

Pour into a blender or food processor, and blend to a purée. Return to the cleaned saucepan and add the milk and seasoning. Bring to simmering point and simmer for 2–3 minutes, allowing the mixture to heat through. Do not boil.

Serve in individual soup bowls, garnish with the reserved watercress sprigs and, if you wish, with toasted wholewheat croutons.*

FOOD VALUES	TOTAL FAT	SATURATED FAT	CHOLESTEROL	ENERGY
TOTAL	19 g	6 g	22 mg	482 kcals/ 2028 kj
PER PORTION	5 g	1.5 g	5.5 mg	121 kcals/ 507 kj

*NOT INCLUDED IN NUTRITIONAL ANALYSIS

eggplant and mushroom pâté

Vegetable pâté is a good, healthful alternative to meat-based pâtés, and makes a filling opening course. The vegetables are high in fiber and free of cholesterol.

Preparation time: 10 minutes
Cooking time: 12 minutes
SERVES 4

1 large eggplant • 1 tbsp olive oil • 2 cloves garlic, crushed
¼ lb button mushrooms, trimmed and chopped
2 tbsp chopped coriander • ¼ tsp grated nutmeg • pepper
2 tsp lemon juice • 2 tomatoes, skinned, seeded, and chopped
4 tbsp wholewheat breadcrumbs
GARNISH
lettuce leaves • cucumber slices • tomato wedges
wholewheat toast

Set the broiler to medium. Pierce the eggplant with a fork and place under the broiler. Cook until the skin begins to split and the flesh has softened. Turn the eggplant 3 or 4 times to cook it evenly on all sides.

Place the olive oil, garlic, and mushrooms in a saucepan, and cook for 2 minutes. Drain off any excess liquid. Add the coriander, nutmeg, pepper, and lemon juice, and mix well.

Scoop the flesh from the eggplant, place it in a sieve and press lightly with a spoon to remove the excess moisture. Place the eggplant, mushroom mixture, and tomatoes in a food processor and process until smooth. Mix in the breadcrumbs.

Place the mixture in a bowl, cover, and chill for 1–2 hours. Taste and adjust the seasoning if necessary.

Serve the pâté garnished with lettuce leaves, cucumber slices, and tomato wedges, and with fingers of wholewheat toast.

FOOD VALUES	TOTAL FAT	SATURATED FAT	CHOLESTEROL	ENERGY
TOTAL	15 g	2 g	0 mg	315 kcals/ 1329 kj
PER PORTION	4 g	0.5 g	0 mg	79 kcals/ 332 kj

pasta and pea soup

A simplified version of Italian *minestrone*, this recipe uses wholewheat pasta spirals which have a higher fiber content than regular pasta. You could substitute any other pasta shapes you have.

Preparation time: 10 minutes

Cooking time: 20 minutes

SERVES 4

1 medium onion, chopped • 1 clove garlic, crushed
2 celery stalks, finely chopped • 2 medium carrots, thinly sliced
1 bouquet garni • 2 bay leaves • ¾ cup tomato juice
1 pt water • ¾ cup wholewheat pasta spirals
1½ cups frozen peas • ⅓ tsp mixed herbs
1 tsp paprika • salt

GARNISH

few sprigs fresh coriander or parsley (optional)

Place the onion, garlic, celery, carrots, bouquet garni, bay leaves, tomato juice, and half the water in a large saucepan. Bring to the boil, lower the heat, cover, and simmer for 5–6 minutes.

Add the remaining water, pasta, peas, herbs, and paprika. Bring to the boil and simmer for 8–10 minutes until the pasta is tender. Season to taste.

Serve piping hot in individual bowls, garnished with fresh herbs if you wish.

FOOD VALUES	TOTAL FAT	SATURATED FAT	CHOLESTEROL	ENERGY
TOTAL	6 g	2 g	8 mg	291 kcals/ 1229 kj
PER PORTION	1.5 g	0.5 g	2 mg	73 kcals/ 307 kj

spinach tomatoes

To retain the maximum amount of vitamins and minerals in the spinach filling, cook the spinach very lightly, until it just begins to soften. Keep a close watch when baking the tomatoes, too. If you overcook them they will collapse and spoil the appearance.

Preparation time: 15 minutes
Cooking time: 18 minutes
SERVES 4

4 large tomatoes • ½ lb spinach
2 tbsp plain low-fat yogurt • ½ tsp grated nutmeg
salt and pepper • 2 green onions, trimmed and sliced into rings
1 tbsp wholewheat breadcrumbs, toasted
1 tbsp grated low-fat hard cheese
GARNISH
watercress sprigs

Set the oven to 325°F. Slice off the tops of the tomatoes, and scoop out the pulp, taking care not to break the tomato shells.

Wash the spinach and place it, wet, in a saucepan. Cook for 2–3 minutes over medium heat until it softens, stirring from time to time. Drain the spinach, squeeze out any excess moisture and chop it finely. Mix with the yogurt, nutmeg, and seasoning. Add the green onions to the spinach, but reserve a few of the onion rings for garnishing. Mix well.

Spoon the mixture into the tomatoes. Mix together the bread-crumbs and cheese and sprinkle on top. Place the tomatoes in a shallow baking dish, and bake in the oven for 12–15 minutes, or until the tomatoes soften slightly. Take care not to overcook them. Serve them garnished with the extra green onion rings and watercress sprigs.

FOOD VALUES	TOTAL FAT	SATURATED FAT	CHOLESTEROL	ENERGY
TOTAL	6 g	2 g	8 mg	291 kcals/ 1229 kj
PER PORTION	1.5 g	0.5 g	2 mg	73 kcals/ 307 kj

dhal

Lentils, which form the basis of this traditional Indian vegetarian dish, are a good source of fiber and protein. Wholewheat Greek pitta bread makes an appropriate accompaniment.

Preparation time: 10 minutes, plus soaking
Cooking time: 30 minutes
SERVES 4

1¼ cup red or yellow lentils
2 medium onions, finely chopped • 1 clove garlic, crushed
1 fresh or dried chili, deseeded and chopped
1¼ pt vegetable stock • ½ tsp turmeric
½ tsp garam masala • salt and pepper
GARNISH
1 tomato, sliced • coriander leaves

Rinse the lentils several times, and discard any discolored ones. Leave them to soak for 15 minutes in boiling water. Drain and rinse.

Place the onions, garlic, chili, vegetable stock, turmeric, garam masala, and lentils in a large saucepan and bring to the boil. Skim off any foam that rises to the surface. Partly cover the pan, and simmer for 30 minutes. Add a little extra stock or water if the mixture becomes too dry.

Season with salt and pepper and mix well. Serve garnished with sliced tomato and fresh coriander.

FOOD VALUES	TOTAL FAT	SATURATED FAT	CHOLESTEROL	ENERGY
TOTAL	3.5 g	0.5 g	0 mg	794 kcals/ 3372 kj
PER PORTION	1 g	0.1 g	0 mg	199 kcals/ 843 kj

curly endive and alfalfa salad

It is easy to grow the crisp and crunchy alfalfa seed sprouts yourself (see the note below), but you can also buy them in healthfood stores and some produce stores. Use them in salads of all kinds as an accompaniment, or even as a snack. Like other sprouted seeds, they are an excellent source of the B and C vitamins, and are also high in fiber.

Preparation time: 10 minutes
SERVES 4

½ small curly endive, torn into pieces • ¼ lb alfalfa sprouts
⅛ lb small button mushrooms, trimmed and thinly sliced
½ red pepper, cored, seeded, and sliced
DRESSING
juice of 1 lemon • 2 tsp sunflower oil
1 small onion, grated • ¼ tsp Chinese five-spice powder

Arrange the endive leaves on a large serving plate or 4 individual plates. Mix the alfalfa, mushrooms, and pepper together in a bowl.

Mix the dressing ingredients together, and add to the bowl of vegetables. Toss well. Just before serving, arrange on top of the endive leaves.

growing alfalfa seeds

Make sure that the alfalfa seeds you buy are untreated. Put about 2 tablespoons of seeds into a screw-top jar, cover them with tepid water, and close the jar. Leave them to soak for about 6 hours. Drain the seeds and put them into a clean jar, then leave them in a warm room to germinate. Rinse them in warm water twice a day, then drain them. The sprouts should be ready to eat in 6 days, when they will be about 1½ in long.

FOOD VALUES	TOTAL FAT	SATURATED FAT	CHOLESTEROL	ENERGY
TOTAL	2.5 g	0.5 g	0 mg	119 kcals/503 kj
PER PORTION	0.5 g	0.1 g	0 mg	30 kcals/126 kj

pumpkin soup

The use of sunflower oil in place of animal fats to soften vegetables plays a significant part in lowering the cholesterol content of any dish. When only half of the vegetables are puréed, as in this recipe, the soup has a more interesting texture and a more appetizing appearance.

Preparation time: 10 minutes
Cooking time: 25 minutes
SERVES 4

1 tbsp sunflower oil • 1 medium onion, chopped
1½ cups pumpkin or squash, peeled, deseeded, and diced
½ lb carrots, diced
2 potatoes, peeled or scrubbed and diced
1¼ pts vegetable stock • 2 small zucchini, thinly sliced
freshly ground black pepper
GARNISH
2 tbsp chopped parsley

Place the oil and onion in a saucepan, and cook over medium heat for 2–3 minutes to soften the onion. Add the pumpkin or squash, carrots, potatoes, and stock. Bring to the boil, cover, and simmer for 15 minutes, or until the vegetables are nearly tender. Add the zucchini and cook for another 5 minutes.

Purée half of the soup in a blender or food processor, stir the purée into the remaining soup, and season with salt and pepper to taste. Reheat the soup if necessary, and serve in individual bowls. Make sure that some of the zucchini slices float on top to decorate the soup. Sprinkle with parsley and serve piping hot.

FOOD VALUES	TOTAL FAT	SATURATED FAT	CHOLESTEROL	ENERGY
TOTAL	13.5 g	2 g	0 mg	396 kcals/ 1652 kj
PER PORTION	3 g	0.5 g	0 mg	99 kcals/ 413 kj

crunchy bean and corn appetizer

This simple vegetable dish, which is presented with style, incorporates a wonderful blend of textures and flavors. It would also make an attractive salad dish for a cold buffet.

Preparation time: 10 minutes

Cooking time: 10 minutes

SERVES 4

½ lb green beans, trimmed

1 cup canned corn, drained

⅔ cup grated coconut • salt and pepper

1 tsp chopped mint • 1 tsp chopped coriander

GARNISH

mint or coriander sprigs

Cut the beans into 2″ lengths, and place them in a saucepan of boiling water. Cook for 3 minutes, then add the corn and cook for another 3–4 minutes, or until tender but still crisp.

Meanwhile, place the coconut on a cookie sheet under a pre-heated broiler to brown. Stir it 2 or 3 times so that it colors evenly.

Drain the vegetables well, season them to taste, and toss with coconut, mint, and coriander. Arrange the vegetables in individual serving dishes, and garnish each one with a sprig of herb.

FOOD VALUES	TOTAL FAT	SATURATED FAT	CHOLESTEROL	ENERGY
TOTAL	35 g	27 g	0 mg	631 kcals/ 2637 kj
PER PORTION	9 g	7 g	0 mg	158 kcals/ 659 kj

melon and ugli fruit cocktail

This is a refreshing appetizer for a summer lunch or supper party and one that you can have ready and waiting in the refrigerator. You can also serve it as a light and delicious dessert to follow a substantial main dish.

Preparation time: 25 minutes

SERVES 4

2 Charentais melons

2 ugli fruit, peeled, pith removed, and sectioned

2 tsp light unrefined brown sugar • juice of 2 lemons

grated rind of ½ lemon

GARNISH

twists of lemon peel

Halve the melons, remove the seeds, and scoop out balls of flesh, using a melon baller.

Cut the ugli fruit sections in half, if large, and mix with the melon balls. Scoop out the remaining melon flesh from the skins and place in a food processor or blender. Add the sugar, lemon juice, and rind; blend.

Pour the purée over the fruit and chill until required. To serve, divide the fruit between 4 tall glass dishes. Decorate each one with a twist of lemon peel. Serve well chilled.

FOOD VALUES	TOTAL FAT	SATURATED FAT	CHOLESTEROL	ENERGY
TOTAL	1.5 g	0.1 g	0 mg	420 kcals/ 1791 kj
PER PORTION	0.4 g	trace	0 mg	105 kcals/ 448 kj

butter bean and mushroom soup

A traditional farmhouse dish, this soup is high in both fiber and nutrients; the butter beans are a very good source of zinc and potassium.

Preparation time: 10 minutes, plus soaking
Cooking time: 1 hour 10 minutes
SERVES 4

¼ lb butter beans, soaked overnight in cold water
1 tsp sunflower oil • 2 medium onions, chopped
2 celery stalks, sliced
½ lb potatoes, peeled or scrubbed and diced
¼ lb button mushrooms, trimmed and sliced
¼ cup canned corn drained
1¼ cup skimmed milk • salt and pepper
GARNISH
2 tbsp chopped parsley

Drain the beans and place them in a large saucepan covered with fresh water. Boil them rapidly for 10 minutes, then simmer them for 35–40 minutes until they are soft. Drain the beans and reserve 1 pt of the stock.

Heat the oil in a large saucepan, and fry the onion over medium heat until it softens. Add the celery and potato, and cook for 2–3 minutes, stirring from time to time.

Add the reserved stock and mushrooms, bring to the boil, then cover and simmer for 10 minutes. Add the beans, corn, and milk, bring just to simmering point, and simmer for 2–3 minutes. Season to taste.

Serve the soup in individual bowls, sprinkled with parsley.

FOOD VALUES	TOTAL FAT	SATURATED FAT	CHOLESTEROL	ENERGY
TOTAL	14 g	2 g	6 mg	635 kcals/ 2682 kj
PER PORTION	3.5 g	0.5 g	1.5 mg	159 kcals/ 671 kj

main dishes

. . . .

When you are presented with a choice of main dishes such as herbed poussins,

oriental chicken kebabs, beef- and cashew stir-fry, and spaghetti with tomato

and basil sauce, it may be difficult to believe that they have been selected with a

low-fat, low-cholesterol count in mind. But you may be certain that they have.

These recipes, like all the others, accentuate the advantages of a healthy eating

pattern. Flavors, textures and colors are carefully balanced to give each dish

that dual requirement, eye- and taste-appeal. Some traditional methods and

ingredients have been modified to satisfy today's health needs without

compromising taste and appearance.

The principal ingredients, used in such a variety of ways are

lean poultry and game – chicken, turkey, and rabbit – fish,

and fresh vegetables, with high-fiber whole grains and wholewheat pasta

playing an important supporting role. Sauces and fillings, so often the danger

area in terms of fat content, have a new lightness and a refreshing piquancy, a

combination that should prove irresistible.

potato-topped vegetable pie

Cook the potatoes whole in their skins to retain maximum nutrients; once cooked they can easily be peeled and mashed. This dish can be prepared the previous day if necessary.

Preparation time: 10 minutes
Cooking time: 1 hour 35 minutes
SERVES 4

½ cup green lentils, washed and drained
3 cups pot barley, washed and drained
1 medium onion, chopped • 14 oz can chopped tomatoes
2 cups cauliflower flowerets • 2 celery stalks, sliced
1 leek, thickly sliced • 1 turnip, thinly sliced
2 carrots, diced • 2 tsp mixed dry herbs
1½ lb potatoes, scrubbed • 3 tbsp low-fat milk
salt and pepper • ⅓ cup low-fat medium-hard cheese, grated

Set the oven to 400°F. Place the lentils, barley, onion, tomatoes (with juice), cauliflower, celery, leek, turnip, carrots, and herbs in a large saucepan and add 1¼ cups water. Bring to the boil, cover and simmer for 40–45 minutes or until the lentils, barley, and vegetables are just tender.

Cook the potatoes in boiling, salted water for about 20 minutes, or until they are soft. Drain, peel, and mash them with the milk, and season to taste.

Place the lentil mixture in a baking dish and pipe or fork the mashed potato on top to cover. Sprinkle on the cheese, and bake the pie in the oven for 30–35 minutes, until it is evenly light brown. Serve hot. A tomato and herb salad makes a good accompaniment.*

FOOD VALUES	TOTAL FAT	SATURATED FAT	CHOLESTEROL	ENERGY
TOTAL	12 g	4 g	15 mg	1314 kcals/ 5572 kj
PER PORTION	3 g	1 g	4 mg	329 kcals/ 1393 kj

*NOT INCLUDED IN NUTRITIONAL ANALYSIS

cabbage rolls

This recipe makes a little cooked chicken – perhaps leftovers from another dish – go a long way. It is combined with high-fiber vegetables in an appetizing and colorful way.

Preparation time: 15 minutes

Cooking time: 1 hour

SERVES 4

8 large green cabbage leaves, washed and trimmed

1 tbsp sunflower oil • 1 medium onion, chopped

¼ lb mushrooms, trimmed and chopped

¾ cup cooked chicken meat, chopped

¼ cup canned corn, drained

2 tsp mixed dry herbs • 4 slices wholewheat bread, soaked in a little low-fat milk, squeezed out, and crumbled

salt and pepper • ⅝ cup vegetable stock

SAUCE

7 oz can tomatoes (with juice) • 1 clove garlic, crushed

1 small onion, grated • few sprigs basil

GARNISH

tomato wedges

Set the oven to 350°F. Blanch the cabbage leaves in boiling water for 3–4 minutes. Drain them, refresh under cold water, and drain again.

Pour the oil into a small pan, and cook the onion over medium heat for about 3 minutes, until softened. Add the mushrooms, and cook for another 2 minutes. Add the chicken, corn, herbs, breadcrumbs, and seasoning.

Divide the mixture equally between the cabbage leaves, and roll up into parcels. Pack the parcels in a single layer, with the opening edges down, in a baking or gratin dish. Pour over the vegetable stock, and cover the dish with foil.

Bake in the oven for 35–40 minutes, basting the cabbage rolls with the stock from time to time.

Meanwhile, place all the sauce ingredients in a pan, bring to the boil, then simmer for 10 minutes. Place in a blender or food processor, and blend until smooth. Reheat the sauce if necessary.

Transfer the parcels to a heated serving dish, and garnish with the tomato wedges. Serve the sauce separately.

FOOD VALUES	TOTAL FAT	SATURATED FAT	CHOLESTEROL	ENERGY
TOTAL	28 g	6 g	136 mg	924 kcals/ 3093 kj
PER PORTION	7 g	1.5 g	34 mg	231 kcals/ 973 kj

mixed vegetable flan

The wholewheat pastry gives a rich, nutty taste to this dish, which contrasts well with the light, creamy filling. Use the pastry recipe for fish and corn pie on this page, and bake the shell "blind" at 400°F for 10 minutes. Allow it to cool before filling and re-baking it.

Preparation time: 15 minutes, plus making flan shell
Cooking time: 35 minutes, plus pre-cooking flan shell
SERVES 4

8″ wholewheat flan shell, baked as above
1 tbsp sunflower oil • 1 clove garlic, crushed
3 baby leeks, sliced • 1⅓ cups broccoli flowerets
1 medium tomato, chopped • 3 tbsp chopped dill
2 eggs, lightly beaten • ⅝ cup skimmed milk
½ cup *fromage frais* or yogurt • salt and pepper • 1 tomato, sliced

Set the oven to 400°F. Heat the oil in a frying pan over medium heat, add the garlic, leeks, and broccoli, and stir-fry for 2–3 minutes, keeping the leek rings whole. Mix in the chopped tomato and turn the mixture into the flan shell.

Mix half the dill, the eggs, milk, cheese, and seasoning together and pour into the flan shell. Arrange the sliced tomato in the center and bake in the oven for 30–35 minutes, until the filling is just set. Sprinkle with the remaining dill while still warm.

Serve warm or cold. A green or mixed salad is a good accompaniment.*

FOOD VALUES	TOTAL FAT	SATURATED FAT	CHOLESTEROL	ENERGY
TOTAL	91 g	19 g	448 mg	1570 kcals/ 6559 kj
PER PORTION	23 g	5 g	112 mg	393 kcals/ 1640 kj

*NOT INCLUDED IN NUTRITIONAL ANALYSIS

fish and corn pie

There is a pleasing affinity of flavors between fresh or smoked fish and corn, the principal ingredients in this tasty pie filling.

Preparation time: 20 minutes, plus cooking fish, and chilling
Cooking time: 35 minutes
SERVES 4

PASTRY
1 cup (generous) wholewheat flour • 1 tsp dry mustard powder
⅜ cup polyunsaturated margarine
FILLING
1 tbsp sunflower oil • 1 medium onion, chopped
1 rounded tbsp wholewheat flour • ⅝ cup skimmed milk
2 tbsp chopped parsley • ¼ tsp ground mace • salt and pepper
2 cups smoked haddock, cooked, skinned, and flaked
1 cup frozen peas, thawed
½ cup canned corn, drained
GLAZE
beaten egg or milk

Set the oven to 400°F. To make the pastry, place the flour and mustard in a large bowl, add the margarine, and rub together until the mixture resembles fine breadcrumbs. Add just enough cold water to mix to a smooth dough. Wrap and chill for 20 minutes.

To make the filling, pour the oil into a saucepan, and cook the onion over medium heat for about 3 minutes to soften it. Stir in the flour and cook, stirring, for a few seconds. Gradually add the milk, continuing to stir all the time, and bring the sauce to the boil. Add the parsley, mace, seasoning, fish, peas, and corn, and heat through. Transfer the mixture to a baking dish.

Roll out the pastry to fit the dish. Cover the filling with the pastry, and make a slit in the center to allow the steam to escape. Pinch the edges to make a decorative pattern, and use the pastry trimmings to decorate the pie top. Brush the pastry with beaten egg or milk.

Bake the pie in the oven for 30 minutes, or until the pastry is golden. A green salad is a good accompaniment.*

FOOD VALUES	TOTAL FAT	SATURATED FAT	CHOLESTEROL	ENERGY
TOTAL	81 g	15 g	130 mg	1741 kcals/ 7305 kj
PER PORTION	20 g	4 g	32.5 mg	435 kcals/ 1826 kj

*NOT INCLUDED IN NUTRITIONAL ANALYSIS

mixed vegetable couscous

A prominent feature of North African cooking, couscous grains are made from particles of hard durum wheat semolina. To pre-cook grains, wash them thoroughly and steam uncovered over a bowl of fast-boiling water for 30 minutes. Spread the couscous on a plate, and sprinkle with cold water before continuing to cook them in this Tunisian-style recipe.

Preparation time: 20 minutes, plus pre-cooking grains
Cooking time: 1½ hours
SERVES 4

½ cup chick peas, soaked overnight and drained
½ cup aduki beans, soaked overnight and drained
2 cloves garlic, crushed • 2 leeks, sliced • 2 carrots, thinly sliced
2½ cups cauliflower flowerets • 3 zucchini, sliced
1 parsnip, thinly sliced • 2 tbsp tomato purée
2 tsp ground coriander • ½ tsp ground turmeric
1 tsp mixed dry herbs • 1¼ cup water
1 green pepper, seeded, cored, and sliced
¾ lb tomatoes, skinned and quartered
125 g/4 oz dry grains (to yield 225 g/8 oz pre-cooked couscous);
(see above) • 2 tbsp low-fat yogurt
salt and paprika pepper
GARNISH
fresh parsley

Place the drained chick peas and aduki beans in separate saucepans, cover with water, and boil rapidly for 10 minutes. Cover saucepans and simmer for 30–40 minutes or until they are tender.

Place the garlic, leeks, carrots, cauliflower, zucchini, parsnip, tomato purée, coriander, turmeric, and herbs in a large saucepan. Add water, bring to the boil, then cover and simmer for 20 minutes.

Add the chick peas, aduki beans, green pepper, and tomatoes to the vegetables. Return to the boil.

Place the partly-cooked couscous in a steamer lined with a double thickness of cheesecloth, or a clean dishtowel and place over the pan of vegetables. Cover and cook for 15 minutes, stirring the grains once or twice.

Stir the smetana or *fromage frais* into the couscous, and put in a heated serving dish. Season and garnish the vegetables and serve them in another heated dish.

FOOD VALUES	TOTAL FAT	SATURATED FAT	CHOLESTEROL	ENERGY
TOTAL	13.5 g	3 g	1 mg	1409 kcals/ 5962 kj
PER PORTION	3 g	1 g	0.25 mg	352 kcals/ 1491 kj

goat fish with shredded vegetables

When it is only lightly cooked, cabbage has a crunchy texture which perfectly complements the delicate flavor of the fish.

Preparation time: 15 minutes

Cooking time: 30 minutes

SERVES 4

4 goat fish, about 6 oz each, cleaned, washed, and dried

oil • juice of 1 lemon • ½ lb carrots, finely shredded

½ lb white cabbage, finely shredded

2 tbsp juniper berries, lightly crushed • 1 tbsp clear honey

4 tbsp water

GARNISH

chopped chives

Set the oven to 375°F. Lightly brush the center of 4 pieces of aluminum foil with the oil, and place a fish on each one. Sprinkle the fish with lemon juice, then fold and seal the foil to make airtight parcels. Place the fish on a cookie sheet and cook in the oven for 20–25 minutes, or until the fish flakes easily when tested with a knife.

Meanwhile, put the carrots, cabbage, and juniper berries into a pan on medium heat. Add the honey, and 4 tbsp water, and mix well. Cover and cook over a medium heat for 3–4 minutes, until the cabbage just begins to soften.

Drain the cabbage and arrange it on 4 heated dinner plates. Place a fish on top of each one, and garnish with chopped chives.

---

hint

Cabbage is an excellent source of Vitamin C, which is a water-soluble vitamin. It is also adversely affected by heat, so it is important to cook the vegetable in the minimum of liquid and for the shortest possible time.

FOOD VALUES	TOTAL FAT	SATURATED FAT	CHOLESTEROL	ENERGY
TOTAL	17 g	2.5 g	294 mg	847 kcals/ 3589 kj
PER PORTION	4 g	0.6 g	73.5 mg	212 kcals/ 897 kj

peppers with bulghar wheat filling

This is a good choice of main dish to offer a vegetarian guest. The colorful peppers have eye appeal, and the apricot and hazelnut filling provides fiber, protein, and vitamins.

Preparation time: 15 minutes, plus standing time
Cooking time: 35 minutes
SERVES 4

1 cup bulghur (cracked) wheat
2 red peppers, cut in half lengthwise, seeded, and cored
2 yellow peppers, cut in half lengthwise, seeded, and cored
1 tbsp sunflower oil, plus extra for brushing
1 medium onion, chopped • ⅓ cup hazelnuts, chopped
½ cup dried apricots, chopped • ½ tsp ground ginger
1 tsp ground cardamom • 2 tbsp chopped coriander
3 tbsp plain low-fat yogurt
GARNISH
coriander leaves

Set the oven to 375°F. Place the bulghur wheat in a bowl, pour over 1¼ cup boiling water, and leave to stand for about 15 minutes.

Place the peppers in a shallow, lightly oiled dish. Pour 1 tbsp oil into a saucepan, and fry the onion over medium heat for about 3 minutes, until it is soft. Stir in the bulghur wheat, hazelnuts, apricots, ginger, and cardamom. Cook for 1 minute longer, stirring continuously. Add the coriander and yogurt, mix well, and remove from the heat.

Pile the filling into the pepper shells. Cover the dish with foil and bake in the oven for 30–35 minutes. Garnish with coriander leaves to serve.

FOOD VALUES	TOTAL FAT	SATURATED FAT	CHOLESTEROL	ENERGY
TOTAL	50 g	5 g	6 mg	1394 kcals/ 5819 kj
PER PORTION	12.5 g	1.25 g	1.5 mg	349 kcals/ 1455 kj

gingered turkey with spicy sauce

One of the leanest of meats, turkey is here marinated in yogurt and spices to flavor and tenderize it before cooking.

Preparation time: 20 minutes, plus marinating
Cooking time: 25 minutes
SERVES 4

2 cups boneless turkey, skinned, and cubed
½ cup plain low-fat yogurt • 2 tbsp tomato purée
1 tbsp paprika • 1 tbsp fresh ginger, grated
1 clove garlic, crushed • 1 tsp ground cumin
½ tsp ground cardamom • 1 tbsp sunflower oil
2 medium onions, sliced • 1 red pepper, seeded, cored, and sliced
¼ lb okra, washed, drained, and sliced • 150 ml/¼ pt water
GARNISH
⅓ coconut flakes, lightly toasted

Place the turkey in a bowl. Mix together the yogurt, tomato purée, paprika, ginger, garlic, cumin, and cardamom, and pour over the turkey. Toss together, cover, and leave in the refrigerator for 3–4 hours.

Pour the oil into a frying pan, then cook the onion over medium heat for about 3 minutes, until it is softened. Stir in the pepper and okra, and cook for 2–3 minutes. Gradually stir in the meat and marinade, and cook for 4–5 minutes. Slowly stir in the water and bring to the boil, then cover and simmer for 10–15 minutes.

Sprinkle with coconut and serve with brown rice.*

FOOD VALUES	TOTAL FAT	SATURATED FAT	CHOLESTEROL	ENERGY
TOTAL	35 g	15 g	280 mg	931 kcals/ 3940 kj
PER PORTION	9 g	4 g	70 mg	233 kcals/ 985 kj

*NOT INCLUDED IN NUTRITIONAL ANALYSIS

beef and cashew stir-fry

Stir-fried dishes in the Chinese tradition combine a small quantity of meat, trimmed of all visible fat, with lightly-cooked and nutritious vegetables – a tasty and healthy concept.

Preparation time: 20 minutes, plus marinating and soaking
Cooking time: 5 minutes
SERVES 4

¾ lb filet or rump steak, trimmed of all excess fat and cut into thin strips • 2 tbsp dry sherry • 2 tbsp Hoi Sin sauce
6 dried Chinese mushrooms • 1 tbsp sunflower oil
8 oz can bamboo shoots in water, drained
4 green onions, trimmed and finely chopped
½ small cucumber, cut into julienne strips
¾ cup cashew nuts
GARNISH
green onions

Place the beef in a shallow dish. Mix the sherry and Hoi Sin sauce in a small bowl and pour over the meat. Toss and leave it to marinate for about 30 minutes.

Meanwhile soak the dried mushrooms in warm water for 20 minutes, squeeze them dry, and discard the hard stalks. Cut into halves or quarters, depending on their size.

Heat the oil in a large, heavy-based frying pan or a wok. When it is hot, remove the beef from the marinade with a slotted spoon, and stir-fry it in the hot oil for 30–45 seconds. Pour on the marinade and stir well.

Push the meat to the sides of the pan or wok, add the mushrooms, bamboo shoots, green onions, cucumber, and cashews, and stir-fry for 2–3 minutes. Stir in the beef.

Garnish with green onions and serve immediately with rice.*

> **hint**
> The shape of the wok is ideal for stir-frying, as it produces tender meat and crisp vegetables. The heat is concentrated at the base, leaving the sloping sides cooler. Food cooked first can be pushed to the sides, allowing raw food to be quickly cooked in the center.

FOOD VALUES	TOTAL FAT	SATURATED FAT	CHOLESTEROL	ENERGY
TOTAL	69 g	16 g	207 mg	1433 kcals/ 5971 kj
PER PORTION	17 g	4 g	52 mg	358 kcals/ 1493 kj

*NOT INCLUDED IN NUTRITIONAL ANALYSIS

mushroom and broccoli nut loaf

With its colorful layer of broccoli spears, this vegetarian loaf is both attractive and appetizing. It is equally good served hot or cold, and freezes well.

Preparation time: 30 minutes
Cooking time: 1¾ hours, plus cooking broccoli
SERVES 4–6

¾ cup button mushrooms, trimmed and sliced
⅛ cup polyunsaturated margarine • 2 celery stalks, sliced
1 clove garlic, crushed • 1 medium onion, grated
1 tbsp wholewheat flour • 14 oz can chopped tomatoes
2 cups wholewheat breadcrumbs • ¾ cup ground walnuts
1 egg • 1 tsp chopped basil • 1 tsp chopped oregano
1 tbsp chopped parsley • salt and pepper
¼ lb broccoli spears, cooked
SAUCE
⅛ lb mushrooms, trimmed and chopped
1 tbsp wholewheat flour • ½ cup vegetable stock
½ cup skimmed milk
GARNISH
celery leaves

Set the oven to 350°F. Sauté the mushrooms in a frying pan with half of the margarine. Drain the slices, and place them in a line down the center of a lightly greased 7½ × 5 × 3″ loaf pan.

Cook the celery, garlic, and onion in the same frying pan until softened. Stir in the flour and tomatoes (with juice), and cook until the mixture thickens. Add the breadcrumbs, nuts, egg, herbs, and seasoning, and remove from the heat. Spread half of the mixture in the loaf pan. Add the broccoli spears, and top with the remaining mixture.

Cover the pan with foil, place it in a roasting pan half-filled with boiling water, and bake in the oven for 1¼–1½ hours.

For the sauce, melt the remaining margarine, add the chopped mushrooms, and cook for 2–3 minutes. Stir in the flour, and cook for 1 minute. Add the stock, milk, and seasoning and stir for 1–2 minutes, until thickened.

Turn out the loaf onto a heated serving dish, and serve the sauce separately. Garnish the dish with celery leaves.

FOOD VALUES	TOTAL FAT	SATURATED FAT	CHOLESTEROL	ENERGY
TOTAL	100 g	13 g	223 mg	1511 kcals/ 6305 kj
PER PORTION	25 g	3 g	56 mg	378 kcals/ 1576 kj

herby poussins

Traditional in springtime, these poussins (young chickens) are subtly flavored with fresh herbs and served with new potatoes and a green vegetable – a light and appetizing presentation.

Preparation time: 25 minutes
Cooking time: 50 minutes
SERVES 4

4 × 1 lb poussins
½ tbsp polyunsaturated margarine, melted
1½ cup dry wholewheat breadcrumbs • 1 tbsp grated onion
1 egg, lightly beaten • 4 tsp chopped dill • 1 tsp chopped thyme
1 tsp grated lemon rind • 1 tbsp lemon juice
1–2 tbsp skimmed milk • little salt and pepper
GARNISH
dill or thyme sprigs • lemon wedges

Set the oven to 350°F. Combine the margarine, breadcrumbs, onion, egg, dill, thyme, lemon rind, and lemon juice and add just enough milk to bind the mixture. Season with salt and pepper.

Loosen the skin over the breast of each poussin by easing your finger between the skin and the flesh. Push the stuffing in, covering the breast in a thin even layer. Shape any remaining stuffing into small balls.

Hold the neck of the poussin in place with the wingtips, and place a skewer through the wings and neck skin to secure. Truss the legs and tail with thin string.

Place the poussin breast side down in a lightly-oiled roasting pan, cover with foil, and cook in the oven for 35 minutes. Turn the birds over, uncover and cook at 375°F for 10–15 minutes,

until they are well browned and the juices run clear. Add any remaining stuffing balls for the last 15 minutes of cooking time.

Put the birds on a heated platter and garnish with herb sprigs and lemon wedges. Serve immediately.*

FOOD VALUES	TOTAL FAT	SATURATED FAT	CHOLESTEROL	ENERGY
TOTAL	70 g	19 g	797 mg	1646 kcals/ 6952 kj
PER PORTION	18 g	5 g	199 mg	412 kcals/ 1731 kj

*NOT INCLUDED IN NUTRITIONAL ANALYSIS

oriental chicken kebabs

Marinating lean meat in a blend of fruit juice, honey, and spices is a time-honored way of flavoring and tenderizing it. In this recipe, the marinade gives an Oriental taste to broiled chicken.

Preparation time: 10 minutes, plus marinating
Cooking time: 15 minutes
SERVES 4

1½ lb chicken breast, cut into 1" cubes
½ lb button onions or shallots, peeled and left whole
MARINADE
grated rind and juice of 1 orange • 2 cloves garlic, crushed
2 tbsp sesame oil • 1 tbsp soy sauce • 2 tbsp clear honey
1 tbsp sesame seeds • 1 tsp chili powder, or to taste

Mix together all the marinade ingredients. Add the cubed chicken, and stir to mix well. Cover the dish and set aside for at least 2 hours, stirring occasionally if it is convenient.

Meanwhile, blanch the whole onions in boiling water for 2

minutes, then drain and dry them. Set the broiler to medium.

Lift the chicken from the marinade with a slotted spoon, and reserve the liquid.

Divide the chicken cubes and onions into 4, and thread them alternately onto 4 skewers. Brush them with the reserved marinade and broil for 10 minutes, until the chicken is cooked. Brush the kebabs with the remaining marinade from time to time while cooking, turning them occasionally.

Serve the kebabs on a bed of brown rice, green salad is a good accompaniment.*

FOOD VALUES	TOTAL FAT	SATURATED FAT	CHOLESTEROL	ENERGY
TOTAL	50 g	11 g	290 mg	1297 kcals/ 5433 kj
PER PORTION	12.5 g	3 g	72.5 mg	324 kcals/ 1358 kj

*NOT INCLUDED IN NUTRITIONAL ANALYSIS

Oriental Chicken Kebabs

spaghetti with tomato and basil sauce

Wholewheat spaghetti has a mild, nutty flavor and a high fiber content. You can, if you wish, combine it with green spaghetti which derives its attractive color from its spinach content.

Preparation time: 15 minutes
Cooking time: 25 minutes
SERVES 4

2 tbsp olive oil • 1 medium onion, chopped
4 celery stalks, chopped • 1 green chili, seeded and finely chopped
2 cloves garlic, crushed
1½ lb tomatoes, skinned and roughly chopped
3 tbsp tomato purée • 4 tbsp water • 1 tbsp chopped basil
1 tsp chopped marjoram • ¾ lb wholewheat spaghetti
(see note above) • ⅓ cup black olives, stoned
⅓ cup low-fat hard cheese, grated • ¼ cup pine nuts
GARNISH
basil sprigs

Heat the oil in a saucepan, add the onion, celery, chili and garlic and fry over medium heat for about 3 minutes, until soft. Add the tomatoes and tomato purée, 4 tbsp water, and half the chopped basil and marjoram. Bring to the boil and simmer for 10 minutes.

Place the spaghetti in a large pan of boiling water, and cook for 12 minutes, or until just tender. (If you are using green spaghetti, add it to the pan 2 minutes after the wholewheat spaghetti, and return the water to the boil.) Drain the pasta into a colander, and refresh it by running hot water through it. Drain it thoroughly and divide it between 4 dinner plates. Stir the olives and remaining herbs into the sauce, and spoon on top of the spaghetti. Sprinkle with the cheese and pine nuts and garnish with basil sprigs.

FOOD VALUES	TOTAL FAT	SATURATED FAT	CHOLESTEROL	ENERGY
TOTAL	60 g	10 g	11 mg	1819 kcals/ 7717 kj
PER PORTION	15 g	2.5 g	3 mg	455 kcals/ 1929 kj

veal rolls

The combination of rice and vegetable filling with a spicy wine sauce makes this a perfect dinner party dish. You can substitute breast of chicken for the veal escalopes if you wish.

Preparation time: 25 minutes
Cooking time: 45 minutes, plus cooking rice
SERVES 4

4 × 3 oz escalopes of veal • 1 medium onion, grated
⅝ cup cooked long-grain brown rice • 1 carrot, grated
1 tsp wholegrain mustard • 1 tsp French mustard
2 tsp chopped tarragon • ¾ cup dry red wine
1 tbsp tomato purée • 1 tsp shoyu or soy sauce
⅛ cup polyunsaturated margarine • 1½ tbsp wholewheat flour
GARNISH
tarragon sprigs

Set the oven to 350°F. Sandwich the veal escalopes between 2 pieces of waxed paper, and beat them evenly with a rolling pin until flat.

Mix together the onion, rice, carrot, mustards, and tarragon. Divide the filling between the escalopes, roll up, and secure with fine string.

Mix the wine, tomato purée and shoyu or soy sauce together. Melt half the margarine in a flameproof casserole, and brown the veal olives over a medium heat. Pour over the wine mix, cover, and cook in the oven for 45 minutes.

Transfer the veal rolls to a platter. Blend the remaining margarine and flour together, and stir into the sauce. Cook for 1–2 minutes to thicken. Pour the sauce over the veal rolls and garnish with tarragon sprigs.

FOOD VALUES	TOTAL FAT	SATURATED FAT	CHOLESTEROL	ENERGY
TOTAL	30 g	7 g	254 mg	908 kcals/ 3828 kj
PER PORTION	7.5 g	2 g	63.5 mg	227 kcals/ 957 kj

hare and prune casserole

Hare is a notably low-fat meat, and one that fits well into a healthy regime. In this recipe the pieces of lean game meat have been tenderized, first in a spicy marinade and then again by long, slow cooking.

Preparation time: 20 minutes, plus marinating
Cooking time: 2 hours 10 minutes
SERVES 6

3 lb hare pieces, washed and dried
6 tbsp wholewheat flour • salt and pepper
1 tbsp dried oregano • 3 tbsp sunflower oil
½ lb small white onions or shallots, peeled and left whole
1¼ cups meat stock • 1¼ pt brown ale
1 tbsp dark muscovado or brown sugar • 2 tsp wholegrain mustard
1 tbsp red wine vinegar • 1 bouquet garni
1 cup no-soak prunes • 1 tbsp cornstarch • 2 tbsp water

MARINADE
⅝ cup cider vinegar • ⅝ cup water
1 medium onion, sliced • 2 bay leaves
8 peppercorns, lightly crushed • 8 juniper berries, lightly crushed
GARNISH
2 tbsp chopped parsley

Mix together the marinade ingredients in a large bowl. Add the hare pieces and spoon the marinade over them. Cover and set aside for several hours, turning once or twice if convenient.

Lift out the hare pieces, and discard the marinade. Dry the hare pieces on paper towels. Mix together the flour, pepper, salt, and dried oregano, and toss the meat in it so that the pieces are well coated on all sides. Shake off any excess flour.

Heat the oil in a large, heavy-based flameproof casserole or saucepan, and brown the onions over medium heat for about 5 minutes, stirring them occasionally. Lift them out with a slotted spoon, set aside, then brown the hare pieces on all sides. Return the onions to the dish or pan, pour on the stock and beer, and stir in the sugar, mustard, and vinegar. Add the bouquet garni, and stir well. Bring to simmering point, cover, and simmer over low heat for 1½ hours, stirring from time to time.

Stir in the prunes and continue cooking for 20 minutes, or until the hare is tender. Blend the cornstarch to a smooth paste with the water. Set aside.

Lift out the hare pieces, onions, and prunes with a slotted spoon, transfer them to a heated serving dish, and keep them warm. Discard the bouquet garni.

Mix a little of the hot stock with the cornstarch paste, then stir it into the pan. Stir over low heat until the sauce has thickened. Taste and adjust the seasoning if necessary. Pour the sauce over the hare, and sprinkle on the parsley to serve.

Serve with potatoes cooked in their skins, or with wholewheat noodles and a green vegetable.*

FOOD VALUES	TOTAL FAT	SATURATED FAT	CHOLESTEROL	ENERGY
TOTAL	97 g	20 g	690 mg	3034 kcals/ 12785 kj
PER PORTION	16 g	3 g	115 mg	506 kcals/ 2131 kj

*NOT INCLUDED IN NUTRITIONAL ANALYSIS

Baked Scrod Provencal

baked scrod provençal

A well-presented whole fish creates a tremendous impression at a dinner party, especially when it is surrounded by a colorful and piquant sauce. You can cook other fish, such as flounder or sole in the same way.

Preparation time: 20 minutes
Cooking time: 15 minutes
SERVES 4

1 scrod (young cod) about 2½ lb, cleaned, washed, and dried
2 tbsp wholewheat flour • 3 tbsp sunflower oil
SAUCE
14 oz can chopped tomatoes
2 medium onions, finely chopped
¼ lb mushrooms, chopped • ⅝ cup red wine
1 tbsp chopped parsley • 2 tbsp pine nuts • 12 black olives
pepper

Rub the fish on both sides with the flour. Heat the oil in a large frying pan, and fry the fish over medium heat for about 6–7 minutes on each side, or until it is tender when pierced with a fine skewer or knife.

Meanwhile put the tomatoes (with juice), onions, mushrooms, and wine into a small pan, bring to the boil, and simmer, stirring frequently, for 15 minutes, until the sauce has thickened. Stir in the parsley, pine nuts, and olives, and season with pepper.

Place the fish on a heated serving dish, and pour the sauce around it. Serve with small new potatoes boiled in their skins, or with wholewheat noodles.*

FOOD VALUES	TOTAL FAT	SATURATED FAT	CHOLESTEROL	ENERGY
TOTAL	88 g	10 g	525 mg	2107 kcals/ 8868 kj
PER PORTION	22 g	2.5 g	131 mg	527 kcals/ 2217 kj

*NOT INCLUDED IN NUTRITIONAL ANALYSIS

baked cod steaks

The marinade of spices and fruit juices becomes the sauce in which the fish steaks are cooked. It couldn't be easier, or more healthful or more delicious.

Preparation time: 10 minutes, plus marinating
Cooking time: 25 minutes
SERVES 4

4 cod steaks, about 6–7 oz each, wiped and dried
1 tbsp sunflower oil • 1 medium onion, thinly sliced
1 canned pimento, drained and thinly sliced
MARINADE
1 tbsp sunflower oil • 2 cloves garlic, crushed
½ tsp ground cumin • ½ tsp ground coriander
juice of 2 oranges
juice of 1 lemon
GARNISH
1 orange, peeled and segmented • 1 tbsp chopped parsley

Mix together the marinade ingredients, and pour them into a shallow baking dish. Place the cod steaks in the dish, and spoon the sauce over them. Cover and leave in the refrigerator for 1–2 hours.

Set the oven to 400°F. Meanwhile, heat 1 tbsp oil in a small pan, and fry the onion slices over medium heat for 3 minutes, until it is soft but not colored. When cool, sprinkle the onion and the pimento over the fish.

Bake the fish uncovered for 15–20 minutes, until it is opaque and flakes when touched with the point of a knife.

Garnish the fish with the orange segments and sprinkle on the parsley. Rice and a green salad are good accompaniments.*

FOOD VALUES	TOTAL FAT	SATURATED FAT	CHOLESTEROL	ENERGY
TOTAL	23 g	3.5 g	368 mg	955 kcals/ 4028 kj
PER PORTION	6 g	1 g	92 mg	239 kcals/ 1007 kj

*NOT INCLUDED IN NUTRITIONAL ANALYSIS

rabbit florentine

Pieces of tender young rabbit – a low-fat choice for a dinner party or family meal – are served on a bed of orange-flavored spinach. You could substitute sorrel, which has an even more pronounced citrus flavor.

Preparation time: 20 minutes
Cooking time: 1½ hours
SERVES 4

2½ lb rabbit pieces, trimmed, wiped, and dried
juice of 1 orange • salt and pepper
2 tsp dried oregano • oil
SPINACH LAYER
1½ lb spinach, stalks removed, washed, and drained
juice of ½ orange • 1 tsp grated orange rind
large pinch ground coriander • 1 cup low-fat yogurt
GARNISH
2 tbsp chopped hazelnuts • orange slices

Set the oven to 375°F. Sprinkle the rabbit with orange juice, season with salt and pepper, and sprinkle on the oregano. Place the rabbit in a lightly-oiled baking dish, cover with foil, and bake in the oven for about 1½ hours, or until the meat is tender. Turn the rabbit pieces once or twice during cooking.

Just before the rabbit is done, make the spinach layer. Cook the leaves in a large pan without added water over medium heat for 3 minutes, or until they collapse. Turn them into a colander, and drain thoroughly, pressing out all the moisture.

Return the spinach to the dry pan, and stir in the orange juice and rind, ground coriander, and yogurt. Season with salt and pepper and heat gently.

Turn the spinach onto a heated serving dish, and arrange the rabbit pieces on top. Sprinkle on chopped hazelnuts, and garnish with orange slices. Potatoes boiled in their jackets, or whole-wheat noodles are good accompaniments.*

FOOD VALUES	TOTAL FAT	SATURATED FAT	CHOLESTEROL	ENERGY
TOTAL	63 g	15 g	468 mg	1257 kcals/ 5240 kj
PER PORTION	16 g	4 g	117 mg	314 kcals/ 1310 kj

*NOT INCLUDED IN NUTRITIONAL ANALYSIS

salmon and vegetable stir-fry

Concerning cholesterol, salmon comes into the "medium" category. It is a rich source of protein, as well as vitamins A and D, and contains two fatty acids similar to those in poly-unsaturated vegetable oils. In this recipe, a minimal amount of fish is combined with a contrasting mixture of fresh vegetables.

Preparation time: 20 minutes
Cooking time: 10 minutes
SERVES 4

1 lb tail-end salmon, skinned, boned, and cut into thick strips
5 tbsp sunflower oil
¼ lb carrots, scraped and cut into julienne strips
2 celery stalks, thinly sliced diagonally

¼ lb broccoli spears, thinly sliced diagonally
4 green onions, trimmed and cut diagonally into ½″ lengths
1 tbsp fresh root ginger, peeled and finely chopped
2 cloves garlic, finely chopped
6 oz can small-kernel corn, drained
SAUCE
1 tbsp cornstarch • 2 tbsp soy sauce • 3 tbsp sweet sherry
2 tbsp clear honey • juice of 1 lemon • 2 tbsp water

First make the sauce. Put the cornstarch into a small bowl, and stir in the soy sauce. Gradually stir in the remaining ingredients, then set aside.

Heat the oil in a large, shallow, heavy-based frying pan or a wok. When it is hot, add the carrots and celery, and stir-fry for 2 minutes. Add the broccoli, onions, ginger, and garlic, and continue to stir-fry for 1 minute, then stir in the corn.

Pour the sauce onto the vegetables, and stir for about 1 minute, until it thickens slightly.

Push the vegetables to the sides of the pan, and add the salmon in the center. Stir-fry for 3–4 minutes, until the fish strips turn pale pink. Serve at once, with brown rice or noodles.*

FOOD VALUES	TOTAL FAT	SATURATED FAT	CHOLESTEROL	ENERGY
TOTAL	112 g	17 g	225 mg	1841 kcals/ 7631 kj
PER PORTION	28 g	4 g	56 mg	460 kcals/ 1908 kj

*NOT INCLUDED IN NUTRITIONAL ANALYSIS

Salmon and Vegetable Stir-Fry

hake rings in ratatouille

This recipe is essentially low in fat. It gets high marks for color and flavor, but has a minimal fiber content. Compensate for this factor by serving it with brown rice or wholewheat noodles and a green salad.

Preparation time: 15 minutes
Cooking time: 25 minutes
SERVES 4

1¼ lb hake, wiped, dried, and thickly sliced
juice of 1 lemon • salt and pepper
RATATOUILLE
14 oz can chopped tomatoes
2 medium onions, finely chopped • 2 cloves garlic, crushed
1 red pepper, seeded, cored, and sliced
1 green pepper, seeded, cored, and sliced
1 dried red or green chili, seeded and finely chopped (optional)
2 tbsp tomato purée • salt and pepper • 2 tbsp chopped parsley
GARNISH
1 tbsp chopped parsley • lemon wedges

Place the fish in a shallow dish, pour on the lemon juice, and season it with salt and pepper. Turn the fish over in the juice, and set it aside while you cook the ratatouille.

Put the tomatoes, onions, garlic, peppers, chili (if you use it) and tomato purée into a large shallow pan, stir well, and bring to simmering point. Simmer, uncovered, for 10 minutes. Season with salt and pepper, stir in the parsley and add the fish slices.

Simmer for another 12–15 minutes, until the fish is opaque and flakes when touched with the point of a knife. Taste the vegetable sauce, and adjust the seasoning if necessary.

Sprinkle the fish with chopped parsley and garnish with lemon.

FOOD VALUES	TOTAL FAT	SATURATED FAT	CHOLESTEROL	ENERGY
TOTAL	6 g	1 g	216 mg	661 kcals/ 2826 kj
PER PORTION	1.5 g	0.25 g	54 mg	165 kcals/ 707 kj

desserts

The dessert course provides an opportunity to complete a meal with flair and style — and, reassuringly, with a minimal addition to the fat and cholesterol counts.

Fruit desserts of all kinds take pride of place — our ideas range from old-fashioned crumbles and cobbler (with low-fat adaptations) to elegant fruit molds and terrines, toasty-brown meringues, and tinglingly-cold fruit sherbet, which uses only the cholesterol-free egg whites.

Bring our versions of traditional toppings — the oaty crumble layer and the wholewheat biscuit ring, both made with polyunsaturated margarine in place of "hard" fats — into your year-round dessert repertoire. Fill a meringue shell with fruit purée instead of whipped cream, and blend low-fat dairy products — yogurt, *fromage frais*, and other low-fat cream cheeses — to make layered desserts and decorative molds. It's easy — and delicious — when you know how.

strawberry terrine

Ripe strawberries held in a liqueur-flavored jelly make a spectacular centerpiece for a dinner party or buffet table. You can substitute other berries, or carry the idea into another season and use orange sections instead.

Preparation time: 15 minutes, plus cooling and setting
Cooking time: 15 minutes
SERVES 6–8

2⅓ fine granulated sugar • thinly-grated zest of 1 orange
1¼ pt water • 4 tbsp (4 envelopes) powdered gelatine
2 tbsp Kirsch or brandy
2¼ lb fresh strawberries, hulled and quartered
DECORATION
½ lb fresh strawberries, halved

Put the sugar, orange zest, and water into a pan, and bring slowly to the boil, stirring occasionally. Boil for 5 minutes, then remove from the heat and allow to cool a little. Sprinkle on the gelatine crystals and stir well. Set aside to cool, but do not allow to set. Strain the syrup into a pitcher through a sieve lined with paper towel, and stir in the liqueur or brandy.

Rinse a 2 pt mold with cold water, and arrange the quartered strawberries to make a pattern. Slowly pour on the syrup, taking care not to displace the fruit. Cover the mold with foil and place it in the refrigerator for several hours or overnight.

To unmold the terrine, run a hot knife between the jelly and the mold and place a cloth rinsed in hot water over the base for no more than a few seconds. Place a serving plate over the mold, quickly invert the plate and the mold together, and shake sharply to release the dessert.

Decorate the dessert with fresh strawberries. You can hull the fruit if you wish, but it looks more decorative and provides a natural element of contrast if you do not.

FOOD VALUES	TOTAL FAT	SATURATED FAT	CHOLESTEROL	ENERGY
TOTAL	1.2 g	0 g	0 mg	2318 kcals/ 9852 kj
PER PORTION (6)	0.2 g	0 g	0 mg	386 kcals/ 1642 kj
(8)	0.15 g	0 g	0 mg	290 kcals/ 1232 kj

citrus jelly

A perfect way to follow a rich or substantial main dish – a three-fruit jelley set around a ring of orange sections and attractively decorated with lemon-scented geranium leaves.

Preparation time: 10 minutes, plus setting
Cooking time: 8 minutes
SERVES 4

6 oranges • 1 lemon • ¾ cup water
1 tbsp (envelope) powdered gelatine • 1 lime
clear honey, to taste
DECORATION
pistachio nuts • lemon-scented geranium leaves

Using a potato peeler, remove just the peel from 2 of the oranges and the lemon, leaving the pith on the fruit. Place in a saucepan with ¾ cup water, bring to the boil, and simmer for 7–8 minutes. Break the two oranges into sections.

Sprinkle the gelatine over 3 tbsp water and leave to soak for 5 minutes. Add the gelatine liquid to the pan off the heat, and stir to dissolve. Strain into a pitcher, and discard the rind. Juice the remaining 4 oranges and lime, then place in a measuring cup and add water to make 1⅓ pt. Add to pan. Sweeten with honey if desired.

Pour the jelly into 4 individual sundae dishes, and refrigerate to set, reserving ¾ cup of the jelly.

Arrange the orange sections on top of each jelly and pour over the remaining liquid jelly. Refrigerate to set.

Decorate with pistachio nuts, and serve each dish on a plate decorated with geranium leaves.

FOOD VALUES	TOTAL FAT	SATURATED FAT	CHOLESTEROL	ENERGY
TOTAL	4 g	0.5 g	0 mg	504 kcals/ 2152 kj
PER PORTION	1 g	0.1 g	0 mg	126 kcals/ 538 kj

Strawberry Terrine

blackberry oatie

This dessert has its origins in Scotland, where the combination of oats and whisky strikes a chord of national pride.

Preparation time: 15 minutes, plus soaking
SERVES 4

⅔ cup rolled oats • 5 tbsp Scotch whisky
3 tbsp clear honey • ½ cup low-fat cottage cheese, sieved
⅝ cup plain low-fat yogurt • 1 tsp grated orange rind
½ lb blackberries, hulled
DECORATION
fresh mint

Put the oats and whisky into a bowl, cover, and set aside for at least 2 hours, or overnight if it is more convenient.

Beat together the honey, cheese, and yogurt and stir in the orange rind. Stir in most of the blackberries.

In 4 tall glass dishes, make layers of the fruit mixture and oats, beginning and ending with the fruit. Decorate each glass with a few reserved berries and a sprig of fresh mint. Serve chilled.

FOOD VALUES	TOTAL FAT	SATURATED FAT	CHOLESTEROL	ENERGY
TOTAL	21 g	11 g	48 mg	889 kcals/ 3736 kj
PER PORTION	5 g	3 g	12 mg	222 kcals/ 934 kj

fresh fruit cobbler

This refreshing combination of both sweet and tangy fruits is somewhat like a hot fruit compote. Topped by a ring of spicy biscuits, it makes a perfect dessert for a hungry family.

Preparation time: 20 minutes
Cooking time: 25 minutes
SERVES 4

1¼ cup fresh pineapple, chopped
¼ lb black grapes, halved and seeded
¼ lb seedless green grapes
2 eating apples, cored and sliced
2 oranges, peeled and sectioned • 1 tsp ground ginger
pinch grated nutmeg • 2 tbsp apple juice
SHORTCAKE TOPPING
¾ cup wholewheat flour, plus extra for dusting
1 tsp baking powder • ⅛ cup polyunsaturated margarine
⅛ cup light unrefined brown sugar • ½ tsp ground cinnamon
3 tbsp low-fat milk • 1 tbsp chopped nuts

Set the oven to 400°F. Lightly grease a shallow dish and add the fruit. Sprinkle with ginger, nutmeg, and apple juice and toss gently.

To make the biscuit topping, mix the flour and baking powder together in a bowl. Add the margarine, and rub in until the mixture resembles fine breadcrumbs. Stir in the sugar, cinnamon, and 2 tbsp milk and 1–2 tbsp water to form a soft dough.

Roll out the dough on a lightly-floured board until it is 1″ thick, and cut it into small circles, using a fluted cutter. Arrange the biscuits in a ring over the fruit. Brush the tops with the remaining milk and sprinkle with the nuts.

Bake the dish in the oven for 20–25 minutes, until the biscuit topping is well risen and golden brown. Serve warm.

hint
The selection of fruit should not require sweetening, but if you wish you could stir in 1–2 tbsp clear honey or light unrefined brown sugar.

FOOD VALUES	TOTAL FAT	SATURATED FAT	CHOLESTEROL	ENERGY
TOTAL	36 g	7 g	6 mg	1159 kcals/ 4893 kj
PER PORTION	9 g	2 g	1.5 mg	290 kcals/ 1223 kj

pineapple meringue

Pineapple rings, broiled until they are toasty-brown and then topped with fluffy meringue, make an impressive dessert for a dinner party.

Preparation time: 20 minutes
Cooking time: 15 minutes
SERVES 6

¼ cup white seedless raisins • 2 tbsp orange juice
1 tsp grated orange rind
1 pineapple, peeled, cored, and sliced into 6 rings
⅛ cup polyunsaturated margarine, melted
MERINGUE
2 egg whites • ⅔ cup light brown sugar
2 tbsp chopped almonds, toasted

Heat the broiler to medium, and line the broiling pan with foil. In a small bowl mix together the raisins, orange juice, and orange rind, and set aside for a few minutes.

Brush the pineapple rings with half the margarine, and broil them for 4–5 minutes, until they are brown. Turn the rings, brush the other side with the remaining margarine, and grill for another 4–5 minutes.

Whisk the egg whites until they are stiff. Whisk in half the sugar, and continue beating until the mixture is stiff and glossy. Fold in the remaining sugar and the nuts.

Spoon the raisin mixture into the center of the pineapple rings, and cover them with the meringue. Broil for 2–3 minutes, until the topping is streaked with brown. Serve hot.

FOOD VALUES	TOTAL FAT	SATURATED FAT	CHOLESTEROL	ENERGY
TOTAL	44 g	6 g	2 mg	1319 kcals/ 5568 kj
PER PORTION	7 g	1 g	0.3 mg	220 kcals/ 928 kj

Apricot Ring Mold

apricot ring mold

With its golden-sunshine color and glistening texture, this is a very appealing dessert, and one that has the hidden benefit of a high fiber content given by the apricots.

Preparation time: 15 minutes, plus soaking and cooling
Cooking time: 35 minutes
SERVES 4–6

⅓ **cup light brown unrefined sugar • 1 small orange**
1 pt water
1 lb cooking apples, peeled, cored, and sliced
¾ **lb dried apricot pieces, soaked overnight and drained**
2 tbsp (envelopes) powdered gelatine
DECORATION
scented geranium or other herb leaves

Put the sugar, a strip of the orange rind, and the water in a pan and bring it slowly to the boil, stirring occasionally to dissolve the sugar. Fast-boil for 3 minutes, and then add the apple slices and poach them over low heat for about 8 minutes, or until they become translucent and are just tender. Lift out the apple slices with a slotted spoon and set them aside.

Add the apricots and the juice of the orange to the syrup, bring to the boil, and simmer for 20 minutes or until the fruit is tender. Discard the orange rind, and purée the fruit thoroughly in a blender or food processor.

Sprinkle the gelatine onto 3 tbsp of hot water in a small bowl. Stand it in a pan of hot water, and stir to dissolve the crystals. Stir the solution into the apricot purée, and set aside to cool.

Rinse a 2-pt ring mold with cold water. Arrange the apple slices in the base, and spoon on the apricot purée. Cover the mold and chill it in the refrigerator for about 2 hours, or until it has set firmly.

Run a knife around the sides of the mold, and dip it quickly in and out of hot water. Place a flat serving plate over the mold, invert it quickly, and shake to release the fruit. Decorate the mold with herb leaves such as scented geranium. *Fromage frais* contrasts well with this dessert.

FOOD VALUES	TOTAL FAT	SATURATED FAT	CHOLESTEROL	ENERGY
TOTAL	3 g	0 g	0 mg	1027 kcals/ 4385 kj
PER PORTION (4)	1 g	0 g	0 mg	257 kcals/ 1096 kj
(6)	0.5 g	0 g	0 mg	171 kcals/ 731 kj

dairy molds

A delicious low-fat version of the French *coeur à la crème,* this dairy blend makes a light and delightful accompaniment to berries of all kinds. It is also good with fresh dates or figs, or drizzled with honey and sprinkled with nuts.

Preparation time: 15 minutes, plus draining
SERVES 6

2 cups low-fat cottage cheese
⅝ **cup plain low-fat yogurt**
⅝ **cup low-fat *crème fraîche* • 3 tbsp warm water**
1 tbsp (envelope) powdered gelatine

Sieve the cottage cheese into a bowl. Beat in the yogurt and *crème fraîche.*

Pour the water into a small bowl, sprinkle on the gelatine, stir well, and stand the bowl in a pan of warm water. Leave for about 5 minutes for the gelatine to dissolve. Pour the gelatine mixture into the cheese and beat well.

Spoon the cheese into 6 individual molds. Heart-shaped ones are traditional, or you can improvise by using ramekin dishes or yogurt tubs covered with cheesecloth and inverted. Stand the molds on a wire rack over a plate and leave them to drain in the refrigerator overnight.

Turn out the molds, and serve the cheese well chilled.

FOOD VALUES	TOTAL FAT	SATURATED FAT	CHOLESTEROL	ENERGY
TOTAL	8 g	5 g	30 mg	559 kcals/ 2373 kj
PER PORTION	1.5 g	1 g	5 mg	93 kcals/ 396 kj

apricot praline pavlova

A spectacular dessert to draw delighted comments at the end of a special meal, and proof that pavlova does not *have* to be filled with whipped cream.

Preparation time: 25 minutes, plus soaking and cooling
Cooking time: 1 hour 20 minutes
SERVES 6

½ lb dried apricot pieces • 1¼ cup orange juice
⅝ cup plain low-fat yogurt
PRALINE
6 tbsp set honey • 1 oz fine granulated sugar
4 oz chopped blanched almonds • oil, for brushing
MERINGUE
3 egg whites • ¾ cup fine granulated sugar

Soak the apricots in the orange juice for at least 2 hours, or overnight. Place in a pan, bring to the boil, and simmer for 20 minutes until the fruit is tender. Allow to cool, then purée the apricots and any remaining juice in a blender or food processor and beat in the yogurt.

To make the praline, put the honey and ⅛ cup sugar into a small pan and bring to the boil. Boil for 5 minutes, until very thick. Remove from the heat, and stir in the almonds. Pour into an oiled tin, and leave to cool.

Set the oven to 270°F. To make the meringue, whisk the egg whites until they are very stiff. Fold in half the sugar, and whisk again until the mixture is stiff and glossy. Fold in the remaining sugar.

Line a cookie sheet with waxed paper, and spoon the meringue to make a nest. Bake in the oven for 1 hour, or until the meringue is firm. Leave it to cool, then peel off the paper, and place it on a serving dish.

Coarsely crush the praline with a rolling pin or in the blender. Just before serving, spoon the apricot mixture into the center of the meringue, and sprinkle on the praline.

FOOD VALUES	TOTAL FAT	SATURATED FAT	CHOLESTEROL	ENERGY
TOTAL	63 g	6 g	0 mg	2460 kcals/ 10403 kj
PER PORTION	10.5 g	1 g	0 mg	410 kcals/ 1734 kj

black currant sherbet

It is reassuring to have a fruit sherbet stored in the freezer, a luxurious standby for unexpected visitors for dinner or an extra-busy occasion.

Preparation time: 20 minutes, plus cooling and freezing
Cooking time: 25 minutes
SERVES 4

1 lb black currants, fresh or frozen • 4 tbsp clear honey
½ cup sugar • ⅝ cup water • 2 egg whites
DECORATION
mint sprigs (optional)

Put the blackcurrants, honey, sugar, and water into a saucepan, and bring slowly to the boil, stirring occasionally. Simmer for 15 minutes, or until the fruit is soft. Allow to cool.

Rub the fruit and juice through a sieve, and place it in a metal ice-cube tray or a plastic freezer box. Cover with foil or a lid, and freeze for 1–2 hours, until the mixture is mushy and starting to set on the outside.

Beat the egg whites until stiff. Turn the fruit purée out into a chilled bowl and fold in the egg whites.

Return the mixture to the container, cover, and freeze for another 2 hours, or until firm. Stir it once or twice.

To serve, allow the sherbet to soften a little in the refrigerator for about 30 minutes. Spoon or scoop it into 4 individual serving glasses, and top each one with a mint sprig if you wish.

FOOD VALUES	TOTAL FAT	SATURATED FAT	CHOLESTEROL	ENERGY
TOTAL	0 g	0 g	0 mg	831 kcals/ 3553 kj
PER PORTION	0 g	0 g	0 mg	208 kcals/ 888 kj

Apricot Praline Pavlova

kumquats in caramel

Smallest of all the citrus fruits, kumquats are a good source of vitamins A and C, and of potassium, magnesium, and calcium. Sliced and arranged in rings, they make an unusual garnish. Their characteristic tartness is offset in this recipe by a delicious golden caramel sauce.

Preparation time: 10 minutes
Cooking time: 15 minutes
SERVES 4

1 lb kumquats, washed and cut into ¼″ slices
1 cup sugar • ⅝ cup cold water
⅝ cup warm water • ¼ cup seedless raisins
DECORATION
bay leaf sprig

Put the sugar and cold water into a medium-sized, heavy-based pan. Dissolve the sugar slowly over low heat, stirring occasionally.

Bring to the boil, and boil steadily until caramel colored – needs about 5 minutes.

Remove the pan from the heat and leave it to cool a little. Gradually pour on the warm water, taking great care that the sugar mixture does not splash.

Return the pan to low heat to dissolve the caramel, then remove it from the heat and allow to cool.

Arrange the sliced kumquats in a serving dish, and scatter the raisins over them. Pour on the caramel. Decorate with the herb sprig and serve chilled.

FOOD VALUES	TOTAL FAT	SATURATED FAT	CHOLESTEROL	ENERGY
TOTAL	0.2 g	0 g	0 mg	1136 kcals/ 4845 kj
PER PORTION	trace	0 g	0 mg	284 kcals/ 1211 kj

rhubarb crumble with oaty topping

Family members who like old-fashioned puddings will love this sticky-toffee fruit layer topped with a healthful and delicious crumbly oat mixture.

Preparation time: 15 minutes
Cooking time: 35 minutes
SERVES 4

1 lb rhubarb, trimmed and cut into 1″ lengths
grated rind and juice of 1 orange • 1 tbsp water
¼ cup pitted dates, chopped • 2 tbsp clear honey
TOPPING
1½ cups wholewheat breadcrumbs
1 cup rolled oats
⅓ cup polyunsaturated margarine, melted
¼ cup light brown unrefined sugar

Set the oven to 350°F. Place the rhubarb, orange juice and rind, water, dates, and honey in a 2½ pt ovenproof dish.

For the topping, mix together the breadcrumbs, oats, margarine, and sugar, and spread the topping over the fruit. Bake in the oven for about 35 minutes, until the topping is golden. Serve piping hot.

FOOD VALUES	TOTAL FAT	SATURATED FAT	CHOLESTEROL	ENERGY
TOTAL	60 g	11 g	4 mg	1439 kcals/ 6067 kj
PER PORTION	15 g	3 g	1 mg	360 kcals/ 1517 kj

summer pudding

This traditional English pudding is a delightful way to celebrate the berry harvest or to utilize a store of frozen berries.

Preparation time: 30 minutes, plus standing
Cooking time: 20 minutes
SERVES 6

2¼ lb mixed berries such as raspberries, gooseberries and blackcurrants
¼ cup light or brown unrefined sugar, or to taste
3–4 tbsp water • about 8 slices wholewheat bread cut from a large loaf, crusts removed
GARNISH
scented geranium or other herb leaves (optional)

Prepare the fruit as required; hull raspberries, top and tail gooseberries, and strip blackcurrants from the stalks. Put the fruit into a large pan with the sugar and water, and cook over a low heat until the sugar dissolves and the juices start to run. Cook gently until all the fruit is just tender – about 15 minutes.

Cut the bread slices to line a 2 pt bowl. Fit the bread around the container so that there are no gaps.

Tip the fruit into the bowl and cover the top with more bread slices so that the fruit is completely enclosed. Place a saucer or small plate over the container and press it down with a heavy weight.

Leave the pudding in the refrigerator for several hours or overnight. To unmold the pudding, run a knife blade between the bowl and the bread lining, place a serving plate over the top, invert both pudding and plate, and shake sharply to release the pudding. Decorate with the herb leaves. Serve with *fromage frais* or low-fat *crème fraîche* if desired.*

FOOD VALUES	TOTAL FAT	SATURATED FAT	CHOLESTEROL	ENERGY
TOTAL	10 g	2 g	0 mg	1188 kcals/ 5068 kj
PER PORTION	1.6 g	0.3 g	0 mg	198 kcals/ 845 kj

*NOT INCLUDED IN NUTRITIONAL ANALYSIS

accompaniments

For many of us there has been a deep-rooted temptation to glaze and flavor vegetables with butter — at one time almost obligatory for taste and presentation. With fat and cholesterol counts now of the essence, other ways and other means have to be found to complement the wide variety of fresh vegetables throughout the year.

As our recipes show, the vegetable dishes we have chosen to accompany a main course are almost a meal in themselves, and are in several cases a medley of harmonizing colors, textures, and flavours.

Take Spanish onions turned in the minimum of polyunsaturated oil and simmered in red wine and stock, or young beets tossed in low-fat yogurt and grainy mustard. Potatoes in a rose-red sauce of tomatoes and paprika, carrots braised in orange juice and spiced with coriander seeds, or mixed vegetables — celery, carrots and snow peas — cooked *à la Greque* are all colorful and imaginative variations on familiar themes.

Take heart. Vegetables cooked with wine, cider, tomatoes, spices, and other ingredients have a tasty personality all their own.

mushroom and walnut salad

This mixed fruit, vegetable, and nut salad, with its sweet and sour dressing, makes a substantial accompaniment to a plain dish such as broiled meat or fish. It could also be served alone, as a first course.

Preparation time: 15 minutes
Cooking time: 2 minutes
SERVES 4–6

¼ lb green beans, trimmed and halved
2 ripe pears, peeled, cored, and sliced • 2 tsp lemon juice
½ lb button mushrooms, trimmed, halved, or sliced
1 small malorosa lettuce, washed, drained
and torn into small pieces • ½ cup walnut halves
DRESSING
1 tbsp sunflower oil • 3 tbsp plain low-fat yogurt
1 tbsp clear honey • salt and pepper

Cook the green beans in boiling water for 2 minutes, then drain them in a colander. Run cold water through them to prevent further cooking, then drain again.

Sprinkle the pear slices with the lemon juice, then toss them in a bowl with the beans, mushroom, lettuce, and walnuts.

Mix the dressing ingredients, pour over the salad, and toss thoroughly. Serve.

FOOD VALUES	TOTAL FAT	SATURATED FAT	CHOLESTEROL	ENERGY
TOTAL	49 g	5 g	6 mg	793 kcals/ 3322 kj
PER PORTION (4)	12 g	1 g	1.5 mg	198 kcals/ 831 kj
(6)	8 g	0.8 g	1.0 mg	132 kcals/ 554 kj

beets in yogurt sauce

A popular salad vegetable in many households, beets have an equally attractive role to play as a hot vegetable accompaniment. This dish has middle-European origins.

Preparation time: 10 minutes
Cooking time: 35 minutes
SERVES 4

1 lb small beets, trimmed and scrubbed • salt
⅝ cup low-fat yogurt • 1 tsp cornstarch
2 tsp wholegrain mustard • 1 clove garlic, crushed
1 tbsp chopped mint • pepper
GARNISH
2 green onions, trimmed and thinly sliced

Cook the beets in boiling salted water for 30 minutes, or until they are tender. Drain them and, as soon as they are cool enough to handle, scrape them. If the vegetables are very small, they are best left whole; others may be sliced or diced.

Mix together the yogurt and cornstarch, and put in a pan with the mustard and garlic. Heat gently, then stir in the beets. When they have heated through, stir in the mint and season with pepper. Serve warm in a heated dish, garnished with the green onion slices.

FOOD VALUES	TOTAL FAT	SATURATED FAT	CHOLESTEROL	ENERGY
TOTAL	2 g	1 g	6 mg	290 kcals/ 1237 kj
PER PORTION	0.5 g	0.25 g	1.5 mg	73 kcals/ 309 kj

paprika potatoes

The potatoes can be pre-cooked and left in the spicy sauce, ready to be reheated while the main dish is cooking. They are especially good with roast chicken.

Preparation time: 15 minutes
Cooking time: 35 minutes
SERVES 6

2¼ lb potatoes, scrubbed • salt • 1 tsp sunflower oil
1 medium onion, chopped • 1 clove garlic, crushed
1 tbsp paprika
1¼ cup chicken or vegetable stock
8 oz can tomatoes, chopped • ½ tsp caraway seeds
1 small green pepper, cored, seeded, and chopped • pepper
3 tbsp plain low-fat yogurt
GARNISH
2 tbsp chopped parsley

Cook the potatoes in boiling salted water for 5 minutes, then drain them. Unless they are very small, cut the potatoes into medium-sized slices.

Heat the oil in a saucepan, and fry the onion and garlic over medium heat for about 3 minutes, until the onion is soft. Stir in the paprika, and cook for 1 minute. Pour on the stock, and add the tomatoes (including juice), caraway seeds, and green pepper. Season with salt and pepper, add the potatoes, and stir well. Bring to the boil and simmer, uncovered, for 20 minutes, until the potatoes are tender and the sauce has thickened. Stir in the yogurt, taste the sauce, and adjust the seasoning if necessary. Serve hot, sprinkled with the parsley.

FOOD VALUES	TOTAL FAT	SATURATED FAT	CHOLESTEROL	ENERGY
TOTAL	15 g	2 g	6 mg	1019 kcals/ 4309 kj
PER PORTION	2.5 g	0.3 g	1 mg	170 kcals/ 718 kj

vegetable tempura

Maximize the color and texture of a variety of vegetables in this crisp Japanese dish. It can be served to complement baked or broiled fish, or presented as the main dish with brown rice.

Preparation time: 20 minutes
Cooking time: 10–12 minutes
SERVES 4–6

1½ cup cauliflower flowerets
2 large carrots, scraped and cut into julienne strips
1 large onion, sliced into rings
1 red pepper, cored, seeded, and sliced
¼ lb small button mushrooms, trimmed and halved
flour, for coating • sunflower oil, for deep frying
BATTER
1 scant cup wholewheat flour • 2 tbsp fine cornmeal
2 tbsp arrowroot • 1¼ cup water
SAUCE
2 in piece fresh root ginger, peeled and grated
2 tbsp soy sauce • 1 tsp clear honey
⅝ cup boiling water

First make the sauce. Place the ginger, soy sauce, and honey in a heatproof serving bowl, pour on the boiling water, and stir well. Leave to cool.

To make the batter, mix the dry ingredients in a bowl and gradually pour on the water, beating all the time.

Toss all the vegetables in flour to coat them; shake off any excess. Heat the oil in a wok or deep-frying pan. Test it by adding 1 tsp batter. The oil is hot enough for frying when the small amount of batter rises to the surface.

Using a slotted spoon, dip the vegetables in the batter a few at a time, and allow the excess to drain back into the bowl. Fry the vegetables in several batches, reheating the oil between each one, until they are evenly golden brown.

Lift out the vegetables and toss them on crumpled paper towels to drain off excess oil. Serve at once with the sauce in a separate dish.

FOOD VALUES	TOTAL FAT	SATURATED FAT	CHOLESTEROL	ENERGY
TOTAL	56 g	7 g	0 mg	1527 kcals/ 6359 kj
PER PORTION (4)	14 g	2 g	0 mg	382 kcals/ 1590 kj
(6)	9.5 g	1 g	0 mg	255 kcals/ 1060 kj

mixed vegetables à la greque

The joy of a dish like this one – a medley of vegetables simmered in a spicy sauce – is that you can use any seasonal produce and blend small quantities of more expensive types with plentiful, inexpensive ones.

Preparation time: 20 minutes
Cooking time: 40 minutes
SERVES 4

2 small celery hearts, outer stalks removed, cut into 1in slices
¾ lb carrots, scraped and cut into julienne strips
½ lb snow peas, trimmed
¼ lb small onions or shallots, peeled and left whole
2 tbsp chopped coriander, or mint
SAUCE
4 tbsp tomato purée • ⅝ cup dry cider • ⅝ cup water
2 cloves garlic, finely chopped • 1 tbsp sunflower oil
1 tsp mustard seed, lightly crushed • salt and pepper
1 bay leaf

Put all the sauce ingredients into a pan, bring to the boil, cover and simmer for 20 minutes, until the liquid has reduced and slightly thickened.

Add the celery, carrots, snow peas, and onions, bring the sauce to the boil, cover the pan, and simmer for 10 minutes or until the vegetables are tender. Remove the bay leaf and stir in half the chopped herb.

Serve warm as an accompaniment to a main dish, warm or cold as a first course. Sprinkle with the remaining herb before serving.

FOOD VALUES	TOTAL FAT	SATURATED FAT	CHOLESTEROL	ENERGY
TOTAL	13 g	2 g	0 mg	438 kcals/ 1880 kj
PER PORTION	3 g	0.5 g	0 mg	110 kcals/ 470 kj

glazed carrots with coriander

There's a special affinity between carrots and oranges – and it's not just because of their color. This is a minus-the-fat version of glazed carrots, pepped up with ground coriander seeds.

Preparation time: 15 minutes
Cooking time: 15 minutes
SERVES 4

1¼ lb carrots, scraped and cut into julienne strips
4 celery stalks, thinly sliced • juice and grated rind of ½ orange
⅜ cup chicken or vegetable stock
1 tsp coriander seeds, lightly crushed
salt and pepper
GARNISH
1 tbsp chopped coriander or mint

Put the carrots, celery, orange juice and rind, chicken stock, and coriander seeds into a pan, and season with salt and pepper. Bring to the boil and simmer uncovered over a low heat for 15 minutes or until the vegetables are tender and most of the liquid has been absorbed. Take care that the pan does not dry out. If it does, add a little more orange juice or stock.

Sprinkle with the chopped herb and serve hot.

FOOD VALUES	TOTAL FAT	SATURATED FAT	CHOLESTEROL	ENERGY
TOTAL	2 g	0.6 g	0 mg	228 kcals/ 956 kj
PER PORTION	0.5 g	trace	0 mg	57 kcals/ 239 kj

peas with lettuce

Thanks, no doubt, to the mass availability of the frozen variety, peas have become an all-too-familiar vegetable in some households. This version of the French way of cooking them gives them a culinary fillip.

Preparation time: 20 minutes
Cooking time: 18 minutes
SERVES 4

2¼ lb fresh peas, shelled
½ lb small onions or shallots, peeled and left whole • salt
8 outer lettuce leaves, torn into small pieces
6 tbsp chicken stock • 3 tbsp plain low-fat yogurt • pepper
1 tsp sugar
GARNISH
2 tbsp chopped mint

Blanch the peas and onions or shallots in boiling, salted water for 5 minutes, then drain them in a colander.

Put the peas, onions, lettuce, stock, and yogurt in a pan and season with salt and pepper. Bring to the boil, cover the pan and simmer gently for 10 minutes. Stir in the sugar and adjust the seasoning if necessary.

Sprinkle with the mint before serving.

FOOD VALUES	TOTAL FAT	SATURATED FAT	CHOLESTEROL	ENERGY
TOTAL	17 g	4 g	6 mg	1021 kcals/ 4240 kj
PER PORTION	4 g	1 g	1.5 mg	255 kcals/ 1060 kj

onions burgundy

You can cook these onions in the oven while you are roasting meat, poultry, or game. They are especially good served with pheasant or hare.

Preparation time: 10 minutes
Cooking time: 1 hour 40 minutes
SERVES 4

4 large Spanish onions • 2 tbsp sunflower oil
⅝ cup red wine • 1¼ cup chicken or vegetable stock
salt and pepper
GARNISH
parsley sprigs

Set the oven to 325°F. Peel the onions, and cut a thin slice from each base, so that they will stand upright.

Heat the oil in a flameproof dish, or in a frying pan, and fry the onions on all sides over medium heat. Pour on the wine, bring to the boil, and simmer for 2–3 minutes. Pour on the stock, season with salt and pepper, and bring back to the boil.

If you have used a frying pan, transfer the onions and sauce to an ovenproof dish. Bake uncovered in the oven for 1¼–1½ hours until the onions are soft and the sauce has reduced and thickened. Serve hot, garnished with the parsley.

FOOD VALUES	TOTAL FAT	SATURATED FAT	CHOLESTEROL	ENERGY
TOTAL	23 g	3 g	0 mg	473 kcals/ 1960 kj
PER PORTION	6 g	1 g	0 mg	118 kcals/ 490 kj

snacks

When the family is dashing in from work or rushing out to another

appointment, it makes sense to have something already prepared to pop

into the oven or the microwave or a non-stick pan.

Golden-brown fish cakes with just a hint of spice, wholewheat pasta

and cubes of fresh fish simmered in a peppery sauce, decorative open-faced

sandwiches topped with watercress and orange, kidney bean pâté, ready to

spread on wholewheat toast, potatoes in their skins piled high with broccoli,

nuts, and raisins — fast-food snacks are definitely, in health terms, not what they

used to be.

Take stock of the low-fat, high-fiber foods available and you will

soon see that fast food can be synonymous with healthful food.

Wholewheat pasta takes only 10 minutes or so to cook; vegetables

such as carrots, cauliflower, broccoli, and mushrooms cook to only-just-tender

perfection, in stock or a steamer, in similar time; oats, seeds, or wholewheat

breadcrumbs combine to make crunchy high-fiber toppings,

and canned pulses come into the instant food category, as our pâté recipe

shows.

baked mushroom burgers

These vegetable burgers freeze well, and can be cooked without thawing first. If frozen, add 5 minutes to the cooking time.

Preparation time: 15 minutes
Cooking time: 40 minutes
SERVES 4

⅝ **cup chicken or vegetable stock**
2 medium onions, finely chopped • 2 cloves garlic, crushed
½ **lb mushrooms, trimmed and finely chopped**
2 tbsp fine oatmeal • ⅔ cup rolled oats
1 tbsp tomato purée • salt and pepper • 2 tbsp chopped walnuts
2 tbsp chopped mint
COATING
a little skimmed milk
about ½ cup rolled oats
GARNISH
1–2 tbsp chopped mint • tomato wedges (optional)

Set the oven to 350°F. Put 6 tbsp of the stock in a pan, add the onion and garlic, and bring to the boil. Simmer uncovered for 3–4 minutes, stirring once or twice. Stir in the mushrooms and cook for 3–4 minutes, then add the oatmeal and cook for 1 minute.

Stir in the rolled oats and tomato purée and gradually pour on the remaining stock, stirring constantly. Season with salt and pepper, stir in the walnuts and mint, and remove from the heat. Add a little more stock or skimmed milk if the mixture is too thick; cook it over low heat for a minute or so if it is too runny. It should be a thick paste.

Divide the mixture into 8, and shape each portion into patties. Dip each one first in milk and then in rolled oats to cover them evenly on all sides.

Place the burgers on a non-stick cookie sheet, and bake them in the oven for 20–25 minutes, turning them once, until they are well browned.

Sprinkle the burgers with the chopped mint, and garnish them with the tomato wedges. Or you may wish to bake large halved tomatoes in the oven at the same time.

FOOD VALUES	TOTAL FAT	SATURATED FAT	CHOLESTEROL	ENERGY
TOTAL	42 g	5 g	trace	960 kcals/ 4044 kj
PER PORTION	10.5 g	1.25 g	trace	240 kcals/ 1011 kj

spiced beans on toast

You can have this high-fibre, high-protein pâté all ready in the refrigerator, and all you then have to do is make the toast.

Preparation time: 10 minutes
SERVES 4

15 oz can red kidney beans • 2 cloves garlic
2 tbsp tomato purée • 1 tbsp Worcestershire sauce
juice and grated rind of ½ orange • 1 tbsp red wine vinegar
few drops Tabasco sauce • 2 tbsp chopped parsley
salt and pepper • 8 slices wholewheat bread, toasted
GARNISH
parsley sprigs

Drain the kidney beans in a colander, run cold water through them to rinse, then drain again.

Put all the ingredients except the salt and pepper in a blender or food processor, and blend to a thick, smooth paste. Add a little more orange juice if necessary. Season the pâté with salt and pepper, and spoon it into ramekin dishes.

Garnish each dish with a parsley sprig, and serve with hot toast. Stalks of crisp, crunchy celery are a good accompaniment.

FOOD VALUES	TOTAL FAT	SATURATED FAT	CHOLESTEROL	ENERGY
TOTAL	10 g	2 g	0 mg	1115 kcals/ 4756 kj
PER PORTION	2.5 g	0.5 g	0 mg	279 kcals/ 1189 kj

quick chicken risotto

A little cooked chicken and a selection of colorful vegetables with rice make an appetizing and filling dish which can be served with a green or tomato salad.

Preparation time: 15 minutes
Cooking time: 30 minutes
SERVES 4

1 cup Basmati (or other long-grain) rice, washed and drained
1¼ pt chicken or vegetable stock • 1 medium onion, sliced
1 clove garlic, crushed • 4 tender celery stalks, thinly sliced
1 small green pepper, seeded, cored, and chopped
1 small red pepper, seeded, cored, and chopped
drained canned corn
⅓ cup seedless raisins • ½ lb boneless chicken, cooked
1 tbsp soy sauce • pepper • 2 tbsp chopped walnuts
2 tbsp chopped parsley

GARNISH
2 tbsp chopped parsley

Put the rice and stock into a large, shallow pan, bring to the boil, cover, and simmer gently for 15 minutes, when most of the stock should have been absorbed.

Stir in the onion, garlic, celery, peppers, and corn, and continue cooking for 10 minutes.

Stir in the raisins, chicken, and soy sauce, and season with pepper. Allow just to heat through, then stir in the walnuts and parsley. Sprinkle with chopped parsley to serve.

FOOD VALUES	TOTAL FAT	SATURATED FAT	CHOLESTEROL	ENERGY
TOTAL	43 g	6 g	171 mg	1765 kcals/ 1845 kj
PER PORTION	11 g	1.5 g	42 mg	441 kcals/ 1845 kj

fruit and cheese on rye bread

Open-faced sandwiches make good sense when time is short, since the filling can be made in advance.

Preparation time: 15 minutes
SERVES 4

8 slices rye bread
FILLING
1 bunch watercress, trimmed • 1 orange
1 cup low-fat cottage cheese, sieved • 2 tbsp plain low-fat yogurt
½ cup dates, chopped • 2 tbsp chopped walnuts
GARNISH
1 orange, peeled and sectioned • lettuce leaves (optional)
tomato wedges (optional)

Reserve 8 of the best watercress sprigs for garnish, then chop the remainder. Peel, section, and chop the orange.

Mix together the cheese, yogurt, dates, chopped watercress, and orange. If you are serving the sandwiches right away, stir in the walnuts. If not, add them just before serving.

Divide the mixture among the bread slices, and garnish each one with a watercress sprig and an orange section. Serve, if you wish, with lettuce leaves and tomato wedges.

FOOD VALUES	TOTAL FAT	SATURATED FAT	CHOLESTEROL	ENERGY
TOTAL	66 g	24 g	100 mg	1549 kcals/ 6518 kj
PER PORTION	16.5 g	6 g	25 mg	387 kcals/ 1630 kj

potatoes in their skins with broccoli

When you want to cook four large potatoes in a hurry, boiling them in their skins is quicker than cooking them in a microwave or in the oven.

Preparation time: 10 minutes
Cooking time: 25 minutes
SERVES 4

4 large potatoes, scrubbed • salt • ½ lb broccoli spears
¾ cup low-fat cottage cheese, sieved • 2 tbsp chopped walnuts
2 tbsp seedless raisins • pepper

Cook the potatoes in boiling, salted water for 20–25 minutes, until they are soft. For a crisper skin, place the potatoes under hot heat for about 5 minutes. Meanwhile, cook the broccoli in boiling, salted water for 8–10 minutes, until it is just tender. Take care not to overcook it. Drain the potatoes and broccoli.

Cut the potatoes in half, scoop out the pulp and mash it. Reserve 8 small flowerets of broccoli for garnish, and chop the rest. Mix the chopped broccoli, cheese, walnuts, and raisins with the potato, and season the mixture with salt and pepper.

Spoon the filling into the potato skins and garnish each one with a broccoli floweret. Serve hot.

FOOD VALUES	TOTAL FAT	SATURATED FAT	CHOLESTEROL	ENERGY
TOTAL	57 g	19 g	74 mg	1376 kcals/ 5776 kj
PER PORTION	14 g	5 g	18.5 mg	344 kcals/ 1444 kj

cod and pasta creole

This is just the kind of dish to serve for an informal supper party or to unexpected guests. Use wholewheat pasta for its higher fiber content.

Preparation time: 15 minutes

Cooking time: 25 minutes

SERVES 4

2 tbsp sunflower oil

1 medium onion, finely chopped

3 tender celery stalks, finely chopped • 1 clove garlic, crushed

1 green pepper, seeded, cored, and thinly sliced

14 oz can chopped tomatoes • 1¼ cup hard cider

2 tbsp tomato purée • salt and pepper

1⅓ cup wholewheat short-cut macaroni, or other pasta shapes

½ lb cod filet, skinned and cubed • 2 tbsp chopped parsley

GARNISH

parsley sprigs

Heat the oil in a large shallow pan, and fry the onion over medium heat for 3 minutes. Add the celery, garlic, and pepper and continue cooking for 2 minutes.

Add the tomatoes (with juice), cider, and tomato purée, bring to the boil, then simmer uncovered for 2 minutes. Season with salt and pepper.

Stir in the pasta, return the sauce to the boil, cover, and simmer for 5 minutes. Add the cubed fish. Stir carefully to avoid breaking it up, and simmer until the pasta is tender and the fish just cooked – another 10–12 minutes. Carefully stir in the parsley. Sprinkle with more to garnish.

FOOD VALUES	TOTAL FAT	SATURATED FAT	CHOLESTEROL	ENERGY
TOTAL	28 g	3 g	104 mg	947 kcals/ 4025 kj
PER PORTION	7 g	1 g	26 mg	237 kcals/ 1006 kj

fish and bran cakes

If you are making these fish-cakes-with-a-difference well in advance of cooking them, take time to mold them into fancy shapes. Children especially appreciate the variation with a helping of baked beans.

Preparation time: 20 minutes

Cooking time: 30 minutes

SERVES 4

½ lb potatoes, scrubbed • salt

½ lb white fish filet, such as cod or flounder

medium onion, sliced

1 scant cup 100% bran • 5 tbsp skimmed milk

2 tbsp chopped parsley • ½ tsp mild curry powder

pepper • oil, for brushing

COATING

6 tbsp 100% bran cereal, crushed

GARNISH

shredded lettuce • tomato wedges • lemon twists

Cook the potatoes in boiling, salted water for 20 minutes, or until they are soft. Drain, peel, and mash them. Steam or poach the fish with the onion for 10 minutes, until the fish flakes easily when pierced with a fork. Skin the fish, remove any bones, and break it up with a fork.

In the meantime, soak the bran cereal in the milk.

Mix together the mashed potato, the fish, and the onion. Stir in the soaked bran, parsley, and curry powder, and season with salt and pepper.

Shape the mixture into 8 cakes. You can make fancy shapes by pressing the mixture into cookie cutters.

Toss the fish cakes in the crushed cereal to coat them on both sides. Brush a non-stick frying-pan lightly with the oil. Fry the fish cakes over medium heat for 4–5 minutes on each side, until they are evenly brown. Serve hot, garnished with the lettuce, tomato, and lemon and with baked beans if you wish.*

FOOD VALUES	TOTAL FAT	SATURATED FAT	CHOLESTEROL	ENERGY
TOTAL	11 g	2 g	117 mg	714 kcals/ 3018 kj
PER PORTION	3 g	0.5 g	29 mg	179 kcals/ 755 kj

*NOT INCLUDED IN NUTRITIONAL ANALYSIS

cauliflower au gratin/with cheese

Use a low-fat Cheddar-style cheese for this updated version of a family favorite.

Preparation time: 15 minutes

Cooking time: 40 minutes

SERVES 4

1 large cauliflower, trimmed and cut into flowerets

⅝ cup chicken or vegetable stock

¾ cup low-fat hard cheese, grated

½ cup walnuts, coarsely ground

1 tbsp wholewheat flour • 1 cup soda crackers, crushed

large pinch ground cumin • salt and pepper • oil, for brushing

TOPPING

½ cup low-fat hard cheese, grated • 2 tsp cumin seed

Set the oven to 400°F. Cook the cauliflower flowerets in the stock for 10 minutes, until the vegetable is soft. Put the cauliflower and stock into a blender or food processor, and blend to a smooth purée.

Mix together the cauliflower purée, cheese, walnuts, flour, crushed crackers, and cumin, and season with salt and pepper.

Lightly brush a 2 pt ovenproof dish with oil, and spoon in the mixture. Mix together the cheese and cumin seeds, and scatter on top. Bake the dish in the oven for 30 minutes, until the topping is golden brown. Serve hot. A tomato salad makes an excellent accompaniment.*

FOOD VALUES	TOTAL FAT	SATURATED FAT	CHOLESTEROL	ENERGY
TOTAL	79 g	20 g	62 mg	1418 kcals/ 5929 kj
PER PORTION	20 g	5 g	15.5 mg	355 kcals/ 1482 kj

*NOT INCLUDED IN NUTRITIONAL ANALYSIS

riviera salad

An ideal meal-in-moments to enjoy in summertime.

Preparation time: 10 minutes

Cooking time: 8 minutes

SERVES 4

½ lb green beans, trimmed • salt

4 pineapple rings canned in natural juice

4 green onions, trimmed and sliced

1½ cup low-fat hard cheese, diced • 12 black olives

½ small lollo rosso or other lettuce

DRESSING

2 tbsp pineapple juice from can • 2 tbsp orange juice

large pinch ground ginger • 2 tbsp plain low-fat yogurt

salt and pepper

Cook the beans in boiling, salted water for 6–8 minutes, until they are just tender. Drain them in a colander, run cold water through them to prevent further cooking, and drain again.

Drain the pineapple, reserving the juice, and cut it into pieces. Mix together the beans, pineapple, green onions, cheese, and olives.

Mix together the dressing ingredients, pour over the salad, and toss well. Line a serving bowl with the lettuce leaves, and just before serving spoon in the salad. Serve chilled, with hot crusty bread.*

FOOD VALUES	TOTAL FAT	SATURATED FAT	CHOLESTEROL	ENERGY
TOTAL	22 g	11 g	47 mg	538 kcals/ 2257 kj
PER PORTION	5 g	3 g	12 mg	135 kcals/ 564 kj

*NOT INCLUDED IN NUTRITIONAL ANALYSIS

Riviera Salad

carrot and corn crumble

An unusual blend of vegetables and spices with a crunchy topping, this is a dish to make now and cook later.

Preparation time: 15 minutes
Cooking time: 30 minutes
SERVES 4

1 lb carrots, scraped and thinly sliced • salt
7 oz can corn • 1 tbsp clear honey
½ tsp ground ginger • large pinch grated nutmeg
3 tbsp chicken or vegetable stock • 2 tbsp chopped mint
pepper • oil, for brushing
TOPPING
4 tbsp wholewheat breadcrumbs • 1 tbsp sesame seeds
1 tbsp sunflower seeds • ¼ cup wholewheat flour
5 tbsp sunflower oil • salt and pepper

Set the oven to 375°F. Steam the carrots over boiling, salted water for 8–10 minutes, until they are just tender. Mix them with the corn, honey, ginger, nutmeg, stock, and mint, and season with salt and pepper.

Lightly brush a 2 pt ovenproof dish with oil. Spoon in the vegetable mixture, and level the top.

Mix together the breadcrumbs, seeds, and flour, and gradually pour on the oil, stirring. Season the mixture with salt and pepper, and spread it over the vegetable layer. Bake the dish in the oven for 20 minutes until the topping is golden brown. Serve hot.

FOOD VALUES	TOTAL FAT	SATURATED FAT	CHOLESTEROL	ENERGY
TOTAL	78 g	10 g	0 mg	1362 kcals/ 5684 kj
PER PORTION	20 g	2.5 g	0 mg	341 kcals/ 1421 kj

fatless sponge

For this classic sponge cake no butter, margarine or oil is used in the mixture. It must be noted, however, that the use of three egg yolks contributes a significant cholesterol content. An electric beater is a great advantage.

Preparation time: 35 minutes
Cooking time: 25 minutes
MAKES 6 SLICES

oil, for brushing • 3 large eggs • ⅓ cup fine granulated sugar
few drops vanilla extract
⅝ cup all-purpose flour, plus extra for dusting
FILLING
⅔ cup strawberry jam • ⅝ cup *fromage frais* or yogurt
TOPPING
3 tbsp confectioners' sugar

Set the oven to 350°F. First prepare the pans. Lightly brush the bases of 2 7″-diameter cake pans with oil. Line the base of each pan with a circle of waxed paper, and brush that with oil. Dust the base and sides of each pan with flour. Shake off excess flour.

Pour boiling water into a saucepan to a depth of 2″, and fit a large heatproof bowl over it. Put the pan on low heat to keep the water simmering.

Put the eggs, sugar, and vanilla extract into the bowl and whisk until the mixture is very thick, and warm. A hand-held electric beater will take about 10 minutes.

Remove the bowl from the heat and beat until the beaters leave a trail in the mixture and it has cooled.

Gradually sift the flour a little at a time into the egg mixture, folding it in with a metal spoon. Divide the mixture between the two pans, and level the tops.

Bake in the oven for 20–25 minutes, until the cakes have shrunk away from the sides of the pans.

Leave the cakes in the pans for about 5 minutes, then turn them out onto cake racks. Peel off the paper and leave them to cool. When the cakes are cool, sandwich them together with the jam and *fromage frais* or yogurt.

FOOD VALUES	TOTAL FAT	SATURATED FAT	CHOLESTEROL	ENERGY
TOTAL	27 g	7 g	707 mg	1753 kcals/ 7440 kj
PER PORTION	4.5 g	1 g	118 mg	292 kcals/ 1240 kj

hint

You can use this mixture to make a jelly roll. Brush the pan with oil, line it with waxed paper, and brush that with oil. When the cake is cooked, turn it out onto a sheet of waxed paper sprinkled with fine granulated sugar. Place another sheet of paper on top and roll up the cake with the paper inside. Unroll the cake when it is cool, remove the paper, and spread the cake with jam or jelly. Roll it up again and sprinkle with confectioners' sugar.

herb biscuits

These savory biscuits, eaten warm, make a good snack to enjoy with low-fat cheese or grapes and celery. They also make a good accompaniment to a bowl of steaming hot soup.

Preparation time: 10 minutes
Cooking time: 20 minutes
MAKES ABOUT 10 BISCUITS

1½ cups wholewheat flour, plus extra for dusting
½ tsp salt • ½ tsp bicarbonate of soda
¼ cup (scant) polyunsaturated margarine • 1 tsp mixed dry herbs
1 tsp paprika • ⅝ cup plain low-fat yogurt or buttermilk
milk, to glaze

Set the oven to 400°F. Sift the flour, salt, and soda into a bowl. Rub in the margarine until the mixture resembles fine bread-crumbs. Stir in the herbs and paprika, and make a well in the center of the dry ingredients. Mix in the yogurt or buttermilk to make a firm dough.

Turn out the dough onto a lightly-floured board, and knead it lightly to remove any cracks. Roll it out to a thickness of about ¾″, then, using a fluted cutter, cut it into 2″ circles. Re-roll the trimmings and cut into more circles. Brush the tops with milk to glaze.

Place the biscuits on a non-stick cookie sheet, and bake in the oven for 20 minutes, until they are well risen and golden brown. Transfer the biscuits to a cake rack to cool slightly. Serve warm.

FOOD VALUES	TOTAL FAT	SATURATED FAT	CHOLESTEROL	ENERGY
TOTAL	39 g	8 g	6 mg	1078 kcals 4536 kj
PER PORTION	4 g	trace	trace	108 kcals/ 454 kj

sweet figgy bread

Not so much a bread as a spiced tea bread which is especially good with cottage cheese and orange segments.

Preparation time: 15 minutes
Cooking time: 50 minutes
MAKES ONE 1 lb LOAF

1 cup (scant) wholewheat flour • 2 tsp baking powder
1 tsp ground cinnamon • large pinch grated nutmeg
1⅓ cup rolled oats • ½ cup (scant) light muscovado or
brown sugar
3 tbsp clear honey • 1¼ cup skimmed milk
⅔ cup dried figs, chopped

Set the oven to 350°F. Sift the flour, baking powder, and spices into a bowl, and tip in any bran (husk) remaining in the sieve. Stir in the oats, sugar, and honey, then gradually pour on the milk, beating constantly. Stir in the chopped figs.

Line a 1 lb loaf tin with waxed paper, spoon in the mixture, and level the top. Bake in the oven for 50 minutes or until a skewer inserted into the loaf comes out clean.

Leave the loaf to cool slightly in the pan, then turn it out onto a cake rack. When completely cool it can be wrapped in foil and stored in an airtight container.

FOOD VALUES	TOTAL FAT	SATURATED FAT	CHOLESTEROL	ENERGY
PER LOAF	14 g	2 g	6 mg	1581 kcals/ 6716 kj

singing hinny

The name of this fruit scone, or shortcake, from the north of England, is said to come from the sound it makes sizzling on the griddle. Don't be disappointed if yours does not oblige!

Preparation time: 10 minutes
Cooking time: 16 minutes
MAKES 12 SLICES

2¼ **cups self-rising wholewheat flour, plus extra for dusting**
1 **tsp salt • ⅛ cup polyunsaturated margarine**
¾ **cup 100% bran cereal • ⅔ cup (generous) ground rice**
⅓ **cup (generous) unrefined brown sugar • ⅓ cup currants**
⅝ **cup semi-skimmed milk**
⅝ **cup plain low-fat yogurt • oil, for brushing**

Mix the flour and salt in a bowl, and rub in the margarine until the mixture resembles fine breadcrumbs. Stir in the bran cereal, rice, sugar, and currants, and mix thoroughly.

Make a well in the center of the dry ingredients, and gradually mix in the milk and yogurt. Then turn out the dough onto a lightly-floured board, and knead it gently to remove any cracks.

Divide the dough into 2 equal pieces, and roll them out to make 9″ circles. Prick each one all over with a fork and mark into 6 wedges.

Lightly brush a frying pan or griddle with oil, and pre-heat it over medium heat. Cook the scone for 3–4 minutes on each side. Serve them warm, with honey or jam.

FOOD VALUES	TOTAL FAT	SATURATED FAT	CHOLESTEROL	ENERGY
TOTAL	31 g	7 g	11 mg	2243 kcals/ 9510 kj
PER SLICE	3 g	0.5 g	1 mg	187 kcals/ 793 kj

bran fruit loaf

It is always useful to have a moist fruit loaf on hand, especially at Christmas – this one keeps well in a tin cake box.

Preparation time: 15 minutes, plus soaking
Cooking time: 1½ hours
MAKES ONE 2 lb LOAF

¾ cup 100% bran cereal • 1¼ cup skimmed milk
1½ cups (scant) self-rising wholewheat flour
1 tsp baking powder
1 tsp salt • ¾ cup seedless raisins • ⅓ cup currants
⅜ cup white raisins • ½ cup (scant) dark muscovado or brown sugar
2 tbsp clear honey • 2 tbsp molasses • oil, for brushing

Soak the cereal in the milk for 30 minutes.

Set the oven to 350°F. Sift together the flour, baking powder, and salt, and stir into the cereal mixture, together with any bran (husk) remaining in the sieve. Stir in the raisins, currants, sugar, honey, and molasses, and mix well.

Lightly brush a 2 lb loaf pan with oil. Spoon in the cake mixture and level the top. Bake in the oven for 1–1¼ hours, until it is well-cooked and a skewer inserted in the center comes out clean.

Allow the loaf to cool slightly in the pan, then turn it out to cool on a wire rack. When it is completely cool, wrap it in foil and store it in an airtight tin cake box.

FOOD VALUES	TOTAL FAT	SATURATED FAT	CHOLESTEROL	ENERGY
PER LOAF	13 g	2 g	6 mg	2080 kcals/ 8850 kj

fat and cholesterol content of foods

MILK AND MILK PRODUCTS	FAT g PER 100 g	CHOLESTEROL mg PER 100 g
Milk, cows'		
fresh, whole	3.8	14
UHT	3.8	14
fresh, skimmed	0.1	2
goats'	4.5	—
Cream		
single	21.2	66
double	48.2	140
heavy	35.0	100
Cheese		
Camembert-type	23.2	72
Cheddar-type	33.5	70
Cheddar-type, low-fat, average	16.0	varies
Cheddar-type, with sunflower oil	33.0	more than 5
cottage cheese, low-fat	4.0	13
cream cheese, full fat	47.4	94
Yogurt, low-fat		
plain	1.0	7
fruit	1.0	6
FATS AND OILS		
butter, salted	82.0	230
lard	99.0	70
low-fat spread	40.7	trace
margarine, hard	81.0	varies
margarine, sunflower oil	80.0	less than 5
vegetable oils	99.9	trace
EGGS		
whole, raw	10.9	450
white, raw	trace	0
yolk, raw	30.5	1260
dried	43.3	1780
FISH		
cod, fresh, raw	0.7	50
haddock, fresh, raw	0.6	60
halibut, fresh, raw	2.4	50
lemon sole, fresh, raw	1.4	60
plaice, fresh, raw	2.2	70
whiting, steamed	0.9	110

	FAT g PER 100 g	CHOLESTEROL mg PER 100 g
Oily fish		
herring, raw, average	18.5	70
bloater, grilled	17.4	80
kipper, baked	11.4	80
mackerel, raw, average	16.3	80
salmon, raw	12.0	70
trout, brown, steamed	4.5	80
Crustaceans		
crab, boiled	5.2	100
lobster, boiled	3.4	150
shrimp, boiled	2.4	200
Molluscs		
mussels, raw	1.9	100
oysters, raw	0.9	50
MEAT		
bacon, lean, raw, average	7.4	51
beef, lean, raw, average	4.6	59
lamb, lean, raw, average	8.8	79
pork, lean, raw, average	7.1	69
Offal		
heart, lamb's, raw	5.6	140
ox, raw	3.6	400
kidney, lamb's, raw	2.7	400
ox, raw	2.6	400
pig's, raw	2.7	410
liver, calf's, raw	7.3	370
chicken's, raw	6.3	380
lamb's, raw	10.3	430
pig's, raw	6.8	260
POULTRY AND GAME		
chicken, raw, meat only, average	4.3	
light meat		69
dark meat		110
raw, meat + skin	17.7	
duck, raw, meat only, average	4.8	110
turkey, raw, meat only, average	2.2	
light meat		49
dark meat		81
rabbit, raw	4.0	71

Source: The Composition of Foods by A.A. Paul and D.A.T. Southgate

index